BLAST OFF!

on

New York Science

Book 4

Second Edition

This book belongs to: _____

Buckle Down
P u b l i s h i n g

A Haights Cross Communications ✦ Company

Helping the schoolhouse meet the standards of the statehouse™

Acknowledgments

The science editors gratefully acknowledge the author team of
James A. Shymansky, Larry D. Yore, Michael P. Clough, John A. Craven III,
Sandra K. Enger, Laura Henriques, Tracy M. Hogan, Leigh Monhardt,
Rebecca M. Monhardt, Jo Anne Ollerenshaw, Lionel Sandner,
John W. Tillotson, and Peter Veronesi.

Photograph of a tornado is reprinted courtesy of the National Oceanic and
Atmospheric Administration (NOAA) Photo Library.

People in Science profiles written by Martha V. Lutz and Richard J. Lutz.

ISBN 0-7836-3230-4

Catalog #BF NY4S 1

2 3 4 5 6 7 8 9 10

Editorial Director: John Hansen; Project Editor: Daniel J. Smith; Editor: Rob Hill; Production Editor: Michael
Hankes; Production Director: Jennifer Booth; Production Supervisor: Ginny York; Art Director: Chris Wolf;
Graphic Designer: Diane Hudachek.

Cover image: © Art Explosion

TABLE OF CONTENTS

INTRODUCTION

Have you ever thought about becoming a scientist? You could study dolphins in the ocean, take rock samples from inside a volcano, or explore the stars and planets with telescopes and space probes. Or maybe you'd like to be an inventor or an engineer. You could use scientific knowledge to create solutions for the future.

If being a scientist sounds challenging, we've got news for you. In many ways, you already think like a scientist. Here's why.

The main job of a scientist is to make sense of the natural world. Scientists find explanations for why things happen. They discover patterns in natural events, observing and measuring as they go. They classify things by their qualities. You do all of these things, as well.

Every day, you do things that involve scientific skills. When you call one insect a butterfly and another an ant, you are using classification. When you bat a ball to your friend or kick a soccer ball at a goal, you are skillfully applying the laws of force and motion. When your CD player won't work and you plug it into a different electrical outlet, you are testing the hypothesis that it is the outlet that is broken, not your CD player. When you check the clouds in the sky to see if it looks like rain, you are using your knowledge of weather patterns and cloud types. When you test out different paper airplane designs to see which one will fly the farthest, you are designing a technological solution. You get the idea.

You might not think much about "science" when you are doing these everyday kinds of things. The point is that the kinds of skills and knowledge that make a good scientist are important to everybody.

About this book

Blast Off on New York Science, Book 4, will help you improve your scientific thinking skills. It will help you to practice and review scientific ways of making decisions and solving real-world problems. You will review important ideas in the three major branches of science: earth/space, life, and physical. You will explore the ways in which scientists arrive at new scientific knowledge. This method includes asking good questions, conducting clear experiments, recording data, and sharing and discussing results. You will also practice designing technology, and you will learn about the ways in which science, technology, and society influence each other.

At some point, your teacher will give you the *Blast Off on New York Science* practice test. This test will give you some practice in showing your scientific knowledge. It will also help you find out what areas you need to study.

Testwise Strategies™ for Taking Science Tests

The best way to prepare for any test is to study and review. These testwise strategies will help you make the most of what you know.

For starters, here are several tips to help you tackle multiple-choice questions.

Tip 1: Read each question carefully.

> You can't answer a question correctly if you don't know what you're being asked. Read each question carefully. Make sure you understand it before going on to the answer choices.

Tip 2: Take a close look at any visual information that appears with the question.

Some questions will ask you about a picture, graph, or table. Don't try to answer the question until you've taken a good look at the visual information.

Tip 3: Read each answer choice carefully.

Make sure the choice you select is the best answer to the question being asked. To do this, you'll need to look at all the choices. Don't just pick the first choice that looks good. There may be a better choice down the line.

Tip 4: Use your understanding of science to get rid of wrong answer choices.

Each question will have only one right answer. By getting rid of wrong answers, you increase your chance of choosing the right one. So instead of blind guessing, you need to learn to get rid of wrong answers before you guess. Take a look at the following question.

1. Jill is classifying sea animals into two groups: "animals with backbones" and "animals without backbones." Which of the following sea animals should go in the group "animals with backbones"?
    A. manta ray
    B. cuttlefish
    C. crayfish
    D. sponge

You might look at the first three choices and not know whether these sea animals have backbones or not. But look at choice D, sponge. You know a sponge doesn't have a backbone. So get rid of D. You now have a one-in-three chance of guessing the correct answer. If you remember that a crayfish looks like a little lobster, you might figure out that C is not a very good answer either. That leaves you with two choices. You now have a 50/50 chance of getting the correct answer (which is A).

Tip 5: Answer every question, even if you have to guess.

If you aren't sure of an answer, go ahead and guess. You've got nothing to lose. If you don't answer a question, you can't possibly get it right. If you guess, there's a one-in-four chance that you just might choose the correct answer.

Tip 6: Don't let difficult questions slow you down.

If you come to a difficult question, try to get rid of the wrong choices. Then make your best guess and move on. Don't let a difficult question make you nervous. The next question might be easier. If you want, you can mark an X next to questions you find hard and come back to them later. Sometimes the correct answer will come to you after you've looked at other questions.

Tip 7: Check your work.

If you finish the test early, don't close your test booklet and stare out the window or take a nap. Go back and check your work.

Here are a few tips for answering open-response questions. These are the questions that ask you to write an answer in your own words.

Tip 8: Look closely at what you're told or shown on the page.

Open-response questions usually ask you about an experiment or problem or picture of some sort. Often, you will be able to find the answers in the picture, table, graph, or passage that appears with the question. You will likely need to call on your own science knowledge, too. But start with what's right in front of you when you're looking for an answer.

Tip 9: Answer every open-response question.

If an open-response question seems too difficult for you and you're not sure how to answer it, write something anyway. You may know more about the topic than you think.

Tip 10: Use your best handwriting.

You won't get any extra points for nice handwriting. But if a scorer can't read your answer, you might get zero points!

Tip 11: Relax.

If you've studied all the material in this book, you should be ready on test day. If you feel yourself getting a little nervous or stuck, give yourself a quick break. Relax—but not for too long. Take a deep breath. Look for an easy question to get you back into things. Then keep going until you are done. You can do it.

UNIT 1

The Nature of Science

Review 1

Scientific Inquiry

From the time you wake up in the morning until you go to sleep at night, you are asking questions and solving problems. In other words, you are *inquiring*. As you go through the day, the world presents you with many different puzzles. Each puzzle requires a different set of questions and a new solution. Science is about **inquiry**, too. To be a good scientist means you have to be a good inquirer. With each new puzzle they see, scientists decide what questions to ask. As you'll see in this review, many kinds of questions help with scientific learning.

What Do You Think?

Do you like to solve riddles? The answers are usually pretty simple when you hear them, but they can be a real challenge before that. Try to answer this riddle:

Clue 1: I have teeth, but I do not bite.

Clue 2: I have a blade, but I do not fight.

Clue 3: I cut through wood, but I'm not a termite.

What am I? _____

Key Words

evidence

experiment

inquiry

model

observation

system

Explain how you used each clue to find your answer, or how your answer explains each clue.

Clue 1: _____

Clue 2: _____

Clue 3: _____

What People Think

A scientific investigation is a controlled study of a natural event. When you answer a riddle, you might not think about how your brain tries to answer it. In a scientific investigation, however, it is important to think about the way we look for answers. Asking the right question is the first step. For the riddle, you might have silently asked yourself questions after each clue: *Why would something have teeth if it didn't bite? What blades aren't used for fighting? Besides a termite, what cuts through wood?* Such questions help you reach an answer.

Scientists ask different types of questions depending on what kind of **evidence** they're looking for. When you begin a scientific investigation, it is a good idea to ask big, open questions. These questions should be based on your early **observations** of an event that interests you. Often, these will be *Why* questions, such as *Why is the sky blue?* or *Why do birds suddenly appear in the springtime? Why* questions are great for getting ideas and focusing your mind.

Let's look at one example of the beginning of a scientific investigation. In the following paragraph, find the early observation and come up with a *Why* question that could start a scientific investigation.

> Last summer, Cliff spent a week with his grandparents, who live in the countryside. Cliff enjoyed falling asleep to the sound of all the crickets chirping. He noticed that the crickets chirped very quickly on Tuesday night, but they chirped much more slowly on Wednesday night.

Observation: _____

_____

Why question: _____

_____

Scientists use *Why* questions to start investigations, but those questions are usually too general to use later on. Instead, they ask more specific questions that can be answered by observing, measuring, or experimenting. These kinds of questions often begin with *What happens when . . . ?* or *How many . . . ?* or *Where are . . . ?* Such questions are smaller than *Why* questions, so they can be answered more easily. Asking these questions will help you design **experiments**, which are investigations that see how things affect each other. Questions also help you explain your observations.

Good scientists are also open-minded. This means being able to change your ideas about how the world works when you learn something new. Similarly, you must be able to ask questions about things that you *think* you already know. For example, most people used to think the world was flat. If everyone just accepted this idea, we might still think that way today. Instead, many people began to question the idea, and they soon showed that the world is round.

Whenever you hear or read explanations of scientific ideas, ask more questions! Asking questions doesn't mean you don't believe whoever is giving the explanation. It means that you are curious and want to know more. If someone makes an observation, compare it with your own observations. If it sounds different in some way, ask questions to find out about the differences. For an example of this kind of questioning, read the following conversation between two fourth graders.

"I just read about a place where the rain is an acid that can burn through metal," said Jessica.

"No way!" cried A.J. "Where?"

"On the planet Venus," replied Jessica.

"How is that possible?" said A.J. "Here on Earth, rain is made of water."

"I'm not sure," shrugged Jessica. "It's got something to do with the fact that Venus is a lot hotter than Earth."

Now, even though A.J. was surprised by Jessica's claim, he didn't say that it was *impossible* for rain to burn through metal. Instead, he asked questions. He compared Jessica's strange idea with his own observations, and this led him to ask even more questions. Finally, Jessica didn't pretend to know why it rains acid on Venus: She left it open for more questions. The more questions you ask about the world around you, the better you'll be able to understand the world.

To answer their questions, all kinds of scientists do "hands-on" work. You know: mixing up messy chemicals, poking at dead frogs, or breaking open rocks to see what's in them. But scientists also need to figure out how things work and come up with ways to describe things that are really small, really huge, or really complicated. Scientists use systems and models to help them make sense of the world.

In a **system**, many parts work together to achieve some sort of goal or reach some kind of balance. The digestive system, for example, breaks down the food we eat into substances that our bodies can use. It might seem pretty simple at first, but it gets complicated quickly. Special chemicals in our saliva start breaking food down while it is still in our mouths. Tiny waving "hairs" line the intestines and move the food through slowly. Cells in the intestines take some substances to use for food, but they leave other substances behind. Other organs, such as the liver, squirt special juices into the intestines to help with digestion. We're learning that the brain gets involved, too, sending messages that affect digestion.

Sounds pretty complicated, right? Systems *are* often complicated. For this reason, scientists use models to describe systems. **Models** describe something that cannot be easily seen, shown, or explained. Models provide a simplified look inside a system, often leaving out complicated parts so that the main idea comes across. Look at the following diagram of the digestive system.

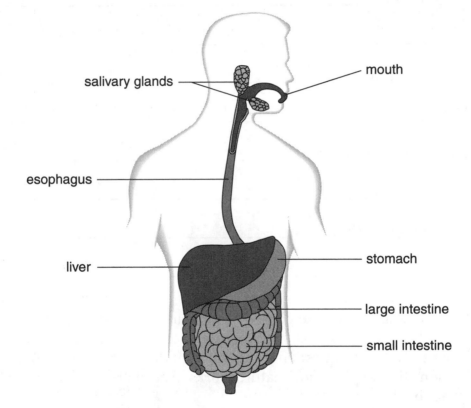

Describe two things that the model shows about the digestive system.

_____

_____

_____

One thing that all types of scientists look for in their investigations is change. You know what change is, of course, but scientists often look for changes that are so small, so quick, or so slow that they might not be noticed. For example, geologists (rock scientists) measure the movement of the continents in centimeters per year! Nuclear scientists work with some changes that are so fast, entire experiments take place in less than a second. In Review 3, you will learn how taking measurements allows scientists to keep track of changes.

What changes are occurring in each of the following events? The first one has been completed for you.

A batter hits a home run: <u>The energy from the swing changes the position and</u>

<u>motion of the ball.</u>

A bird egg hatches: _____

_____

A fire burns in a fireplace: _____

_____

The Moon rises in the evening: _____

_____

Thunder rumbles in the sky: _____

_____

You can explore changes that take place over time in your own experiments by coming up with testable questions, making careful observations, and keeping track of what happens. By asking questions that help you decide how to go on, you can run investigations that explore how nature works. And that, after all, is what science is all about.

Using What You Know

Your teacher has a problem that needs solving. There are four cans of soup in the cupboard. All four cans are the same size. Two of the cans contain chicken noodle soup. The other two contain cream of mushroom soup. The labels on one of the chicken noodle soup cans and one of the cream of mushroom soup cans were accidentally torn off. How can the contents of these cans be identified without opening or shaking them?

Step 1: Your teacher will give you two labeled cans of soup and a board to use as a ramp. Use data on how the cans roll to help you solve the problem of the missing labels.

Before you do any tests, which can of soup do you think will roll faster? Why do you think so?

_____

_____

_____

How will you determine which can rolls faster?

_____

_____

_____

Which can rolled faster down the ramp?

_____

Step 2: Now your teacher will give you two unmarked cans. One can is chicken noodle soup, and the other is cream of mushroom soup.

Without opening them, what can you do to figure out which can is which?

_____

_____

_____

Why do you think this will work?

_____

_____

_____

Think It Over

1. What evidence (observations, measurements, information, or data) is similar for the chicken noodle soup can and the cream of mushroom soup can?

   _____

   _____

   _____

2. What is the major difference between the chicken noodle soup and the cream of mushroom soup? What evidence did you use to make this claim?

   _____

   _____

   _____

3. Lacey said that she figured out which can rolled faster. She did this by placing one can right behind the other and rolling them both down the ramp. Is this a good way of conducting the experiment? Why or why not?

   _____

   _____

   _____

4. If you had the same four cans (two of each), but this time *three* of them had the labels peeled off, could you figure out which ones were which? How would you do it?

   _____

   _____

   _____

Practice Questions

1. The Sun and the group of objects orbiting it affect each other. What is this an example of?

   A. a system   C. an explanation

   B. evidence   D. a model

2. Mr. Spezio used a globe to show his fourth-grade class where the oceans and continents are. What is this an example of?

   A. a system   C. evidence

   B. a model   D. an invention

Directions: Use the following paragraph and diagram to answer Numbers 3 and 4.

Adriana placed a beaker upside down over a water plant in an aquarium. After several weeks, she observed that the water level in the beaker had dropped.

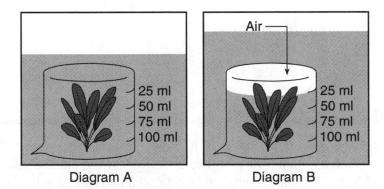

Diagram A   Diagram B

3. Adriana's experiment can be used to address which of the following questions?

   A. Which plant food works best?

   B. How much water can most beakers hold?

   C. Do water plants produce any gas over time?

   D. Can plants survive if they are put into ice-cold water?

4. What are two changes that are occurring during Adriana's experiment?

   _____

   _____

   _____

   _____

5. Give an example for each of the following scientific ideas:

a. Model: _____

_____

_____

b. System: _____

_____

_____

c. Change: _____

_____

_____

People in Science

Pity Robert Hooke. He was an English experimental scientist who discovered elements of the law of gravitation before the very famous Sir Isaac Newton made similar discoveries. But Hooke lacked Newton's math skills and never could demonstrate the theory. Still, Hooke did put his name in the science books. He studied how gases behave and discovered the details of how things burn. He built an early version of a reflecting telescope and invented and improved tools used in meteorology. He discovered plant cells through the use of a microscope and studied fossils. And he developed the theory of *Hooke's Law*. What's Hooke's Law, you ask? It states that an elastic body bends or stretches out of shape in direct proportion to the force acting upon it. Hooke was a virtuoso scientist—his interests took him to all areas of science.

Robert Hooke
(England 1635–1703)

Review 2

Scientific Investigations

Everywhere we look, there are **patterns** in nature. Day turns to night and night becomes day, over and over again. Babies are born, grow into children, and then become adults, who then often have children of their own. Understanding the patterns in nature can help you make predictions about what will happen next. As you learned in Review 1, asking questions helps us learn about the natural world. In this review, you will learn how to recognize scientific information, to tell the difference between fact and opinion, and to run your own scientific investigations.

What Do You Think?

For their science project, Alan and Tamisha watched robins build nests. In his report to the class, Alan said that robins repair and use the old nests of other birds. Tamisha, on the other hand, said that robins use grass, twigs, and paper scraps to build new nests.

How would you decide which classmate to believe?

_____

_____

_____

_____

Key Words

claim

data

evidence

fact

global warming

greenhouse effect

hypothesis

judgment

opinion

pattern

research

variable

When a person makes a statement he or she wants us to believe is true, that statement is called a **claim**.

How do scientists decide whether to believe what another scientist claims?

_____

_____

_____

_____

What People Think

Imagine two TV commercials: Two juice companies, Fruitiest Fruit Juice and SlurpyGood Fruit Juice, are trying to sell you their juice. Both companies claim that their juice is the healthiest fruit juice you can buy. Is either fruit juice really the healthiest one you can buy? We have to make **judgments** like these all the time. When you make a judgment, you decide what the best action or opinion is. Sometimes it can be hard to decide what to do or believe.

If you are trying to judge which of the two juices is healthier, what should you do to get information that will help you decide?

_____

_____

_____

_____

Like you, scientists must also make judgments and decisions. They base their judgments and decisions on the **evidence**, or clues, they have gathered. They also make judgments based on what they have learned from past studies by other scientists. Most important, they rely on the claims of others only if those claims are based on solid evidence.

Scientists, then, do the same thing you do when you sort out facts from opinions. A **fact** is a piece of information that can be proven to be true. We say that facts have been *established*, which means that they have been proven again and again. **Opinions**, on the other hand, cannot be proven; they are statements about one's personal feelings. Opinions are important, but they cannot be the basis of scientific knowledge.

Read the following statements. On the lines provided, write down whether they are facts or opinions, and explain your decisions.

Temperatures at the North Pole in 2002 were the highest since temperature data have been recorded.

_____

_____

Global warming is a result of people's greed and lack of ability to plan for future generations.

_____

_____

As you learned in Review 1, an important step in scientific investigations is coming up with the right question to ask. Good questions help scientists focus their investigations. A **hypothesis** (the singular form of *hypotheses*) is a question or a statement about the natural world that can be scientifically tested. It is important to note that a hypothesis must be *testable* to be valid, but it doesn't necessarily have to be *correct*. A hypothesis is only invalid if it is not testable.

Are the following hypotheses valid or invalid? Explain why.

The average heartbeat of a hobbit at rest is 52 beats per minute.

_____

_____

Grasshoppers chirp more frequently as the temperature rises.

_____

_____

The Earth is flat.

_____

_____

In an investigation, a scientist will often change the hypothesis after observing the first set of results. The new hypothesis might lead to a different type of investigation, which produces new **data**, or information. Again, the new results are compared to the hypothesis, and the hypothesis might be changed a second time. This cycle can repeat itself many times, until the scientist finds a hypothesis that predicts the results of the investigation. In this way, "incorrect" hypotheses can still help an investigation by helping investigators improve their ideas.

Scientists must often change their hypotheses and repeat experiments because they encounter variables. **Variables** are things that can change the results of an experiment. Every day, people try to control variables to stop things from changing. They do this to make things safer or more enjoyable. For example, many kinds of food would spoil if they were not placed in the refrigerator. Also, chemicals are often added to foods to keep the foods from spoiling. Just like human beings, bacteria and molds have certain things they need to grow. Most bacteria and molds grow best in a warm place.

> What variable are we controlling when we place food in a refrigerator? How do you think refrigeration affects mold or bacteria growth?

_____

_____

_____

Let's take a look at the whole process. The following diagram shows the steps in a typical scientific investigation. Not all investigations follow these steps, but the diagram shows the general pattern for most investigations.

A Scientific Investigation

1. Observe and generalize
2. Ask a question
3. Form a hypothesis   3. Change hypothesis
4. Make a prediction   4. Make a prediction
5. Experiment and observe   5. Experiment and observe

Repeat steps 3–5 until prediction matches observation, then . . .

6. Report findings

You have already learned about the first three steps: observing natural events and making general statements about them, asking broad questions about the event to focus your mind, and coming up with a testable hypothesis. Science is all about finding the patterns in nature, so you want to end up with a hypothesis that can make predictions about those patterns. That's what step 4 is about: Make a prediction based on what you think will happen. In step 5, you run an experiment and see whether your prediction was correct.

Most experiments will show that the first hypothesis did not predict things perfectly. This is normal. In that case, you change your hypothesis to fit the new observations and then run the experiment again. The best scientific investigations go through this process many times. Repeating experiments is the only way to get hypotheses that work really well at predicting natural patterns.

> Hank formed the following hypothesis: "Magnets attract metal objects." During his experiment, however, Hank found that magnets do not attract aluminum cans or copper wire. How would you change Hank's hypothesis to continue the investigation?

_____

_____

_____

_____

During an experiment, it is important to observe things very carefully. Careful observation includes measuring changes; you will learn more about this in Review 3. During and after the experiment, good scientific inquiry asks you to understand what you see, make a conclusion, and report the results. This last step is very important: Scientists are constantly asking themselves and other scientists, "How do you know that?" or "How does your evidence support your conclusion?" Sharing information is the only way to be sure. You'll learn many ways to share your results in Review 4.

Many scientists are extremely smart, but none of them can do their work all alone. All scientists look for information and help from each other through **research**. Sometimes this simply means they will talk with their partners, or maybe they'll call up a teacher they once had. Usually, it means they will read as many reports as possible on whatever subject they're working on. Some scientists spend as much time in the library as they do in their laboratories!

Imagine that you've decided to learn as much as you can about elephants. Where would you start? Describe how you could use each of the following sources to help you learn more about elephants.

Your science teacher: _____

_____

The Internet: _____

_____

The local zoo: _____

_____

An encyclopedia: _____

_____

The book, *The Mammals of Africa*: _____

_____

Using What You Know

One issue that scientists are investigating is the rising average world temperature, called **global warming**. Scientists think that certain gases in the air have caused this warming trend. How do gases cause global warming? Much of the Sun's energy that enters the Earth's atmosphere bounces back out into space. However, some gases in the atmosphere trap some of this heat near the Earth. They act like the closed windows of a car, raising the temperature inside. This is called the **greenhouse effect**.

In this activity, you will build a model to compare the temperature of two different systems. You will use a light for a heat source. Your teacher will provide you and a partner with the materials you will need to run an experiment.

Step 1: Use a separate piece of paper or a notebook to create a science journal for this activity. In your journal, list the materials provided by your teacher.

Step 2: Together with a partner, create a step-by-step procedure to find out how the temperature of a *closed* system compares with the temperature of an *open* system after being heated for a period of time. Do not start the experiment; just record your steps in your journal.

Step 3: Share your plans with the rest of the class. Discuss each other's plans, trying to find out the best way to go ahead with the experiment. Rewrite your plans in your journal.

Step 4: Using the materials provided by your teacher, follow the plans that you and your partner created to test the greenhouse effect.

Step 5: In your journal, record your results. Use numbers, words, and drawings whenever you think they are needed.

Think It Over

1. What was your hypothesis on what will happen during your experiment?

    _____

    _____

    _____

2. Based on your results, what adjustment would you make to your hypothesis?

    _____

    _____

    _____

3. Which cup of soil had the greater temperature change during the experiment? Explain your answer.

    _____

    Why do you think this happened?

    _____

    _____

    _____

4. What is one difference between your model and the Earth system you are modeling?

    _____

    _____

    _____

Practice Questions

Directions: The following diagrams show a patch of sunlight on the floor at two times of the day in the United States. Use this information to answer Numbers 1 and 2.

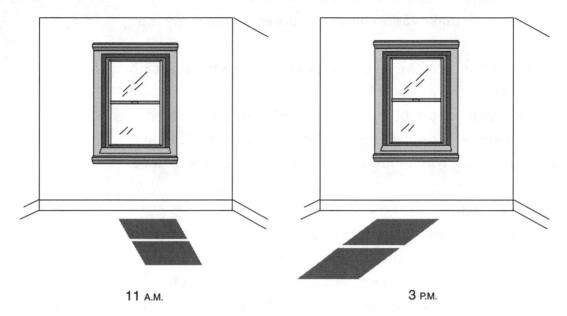

11 A.M.   3 P.M.

1. What natural pattern caused the patch of sunlight to change positions?
    A. The Earth spins from west to east.
    B. The Earth travels around the Sun.
    C. The Moon travels around the Earth.
    D. The Sun circles the Earth once each day.

2. In the blank diagram shown here, draw where you think the patch of sunlight will be at 5 P.M.

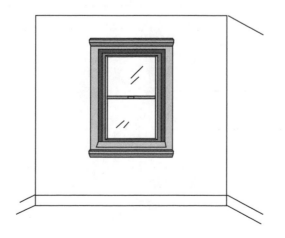

3. Scientists explore questions that can be answered with facts. Which of the following is not a scientific question that a scientist might try to answer?

   A. How many frogs are in a pond?

   B. How do birds learn their "songs"?

   C. Are skateboards more fun than bicycles?

   D. Are earthquakes and volcanoes caused by the same thing?

4. Which of the following is the best example of a hypothesis?

   A. Owls are the meanest birds in all the forest.

   B. The speed of a rabbit and its diet are somehow related.

   C. Einstein was probably the smartest scientist of all time.

   D. There is no way to improve the way that science is done.

5. What is a claim?

   A. a law of nature that everyone knows

   B. a clue that helps you solve a problem

   C. a statement that someone wants you to believe is true

   D. an animal with a two-piece shell that lives in the water

6. A claim is given below. Tell what you think about the accuracy of this claim and why you think that way.

If a black cat crosses your path, you will have bad luck.

_____

_____

_____

_____

Review 3

Observing and Measuring

Before starting their experiments, scientists almost always research the question they are about to test. They read books and articles, and they speak with other scientists who might be able to help. Not all of the information a scientist uncovers is useful. Scientists must judge what information will be important for their experiments, and what information they should ignore. When they run the actual experiments, scientists collect their data in the same way that you do—by using their five senses. This is usually not enough, though. To extend their senses, scientists learn to use many different instruments. Scientists also take many measurements during an experiment, sometimes measuring the same thing over and over. They do this to be sure that their data are as accurate as possible and to reduce errors in their findings.

This process may sound hard, but it can be creative and fun, too. Are you ready to collect data like a scientist?

Key Words

data	graduated cylinder	U.S. customary system
error	instrument	variable
fair test	metric system	

What Do You Think?

To solve problems and make good decisions, you have to start with good information—or what scientists call **data**. How could you go about collecting data on the following?

The distance from your home to school: _____

The time it takes to walk to school: _____

The tallest person in your class: _____

The heaviest book in your classroom: _____

The loudest noise at school yesterday: _____

The healthiest food served at lunch today: _____

What People Think

To collect data like a scientist, you must make measurements. By measuring things, you can put them into mathematical terms. Math is like a language that anyone can understand. If we use numbers to describe our world, we make sure that anyone who reads our results thinks of them in roughly the same way. If you call a boat *huge*, for example, someone might imagine anything from a rowboat to an ocean liner. But if you said that the boat was 110 meters long, then people would know exactly how long the boat was.

Here is an example to show why it is important to use mathematical language to describe observations. Mandy and her classmate Felix were observing an icicle that formed outside their classroom window to see whether the icicle would grow or shrink over the next few days. On Monday, they made their first observations and wrote them down in a journal. On Tuesday, they made another set of observations and compared their findings. Surprisingly, Felix thought the icicle shrank, but Mandy thought it grew. Neither of them used measurements to describe their observations.

Why do you think that Mandy and Felix observed different things?

_____

_____

_____

By themselves, human senses are not very reliable for scientific observations. Our senses can play tricks on us in many ways; that's why measuring is so important. If Mandy and Felix get the chance to observe another icicle, they'll measure its changes, day by day. This way, they'll have an easier time figuring out what happens to it.

Taking good measurements also allows us to keep track of the **variables**, which are the factors in an experiment that can change. (The word *variable* relates to the word *vary*, which means "to change.") The best kind of experiments are **fair tests**, which test one variable and try to keep all the other variables the same. You must keep the conditions the same every time the experiment is repeated; this is the only way you can compare the results in a fair way. For example, if you were testing how fast different bicycles were, you'd have to control the variables—in this case, the rider and the racetrack. That means the same rider would ride the bicycles that you were testing on the same racetrack.

Wilton wants to test three different kinds of plant food to see which one will cause his tomato plants to produce the most fruit. What variable is Wilton testing?

_____

What would be a fair test to find out which plant food produces the most fruit?

_____

_____

_____

In science, a fair test usually involves doing an experiment more than once. Repeating an experiment helps you judge your experiments correctly. In other words, if an unusual event happens during any one test, you will know that the event is unusual because you can compare it to the other times you ran the test. Repeating tests gives you a chance to see a pattern.

Why should Wilton grow many tomato plants with each type of food instead of just one?

_____

_____

_____

Measurements are very important in science because science is about observing natural events and looking for patterns in data. Measurements allow us to make sure that our observations are correct. For precise measurements, you need to use measuring **instruments** such as metersticks, balances, stopwatches, and so on. But measurements are never exact. Any measurement always has some amount of **error**. For example, if someone wanted to know how tall you are, you could stand against the wall, make a mark at the top of your head, and then measure the height with a meterstick. The measurement would be close to your real height, but it would probably not be exact.

How could an error be made in measuring your height this way?

_____

_____

Because most measurements involve a small amount of error, it is extremely important to take more than one measurement. Multiple measurements can be checked against each other to show which ones are most precise. This is one reason why scientists prefer multiple sources of data, and why experiments need to be repeated many times before their results can be accepted.

When you use a measuring tool, you need to know what unit of measurement it uses. You need to remember two major systems of measurement:

(1) The **metric system** is the most common system in the world for making measurements. The basic units in the metric system are the meter for length, the kilogram for weight, and the liter for volume (the amount of space something takes up).

(2) The **U.S. customary system** was developed by scientists in England, so its units are often called *English units*. This system is used by most people in the United States, but most scientists in the United States use the metric system. You're probably familiar with this system, which uses inches, feet, gallons, ounces, and pounds.

Using What You Know

Step 1: How tall are you?

Your teacher will give you a meterstick for this activity.

Estimate your height in centimeters (cm).

Record your estimate here: _____ cm

Have three people in your group use a meterstick to measure your height (in cm). Record the measurements in the spaces below. Don't peek at each other's measurements; just record whatever each person gets.

_____ cm   _____ cm   _____ cm

Step 2: What is the mass of a pencil?

Your teacher will give you a gram balance for this activity.

Estimate the mass of a pencil in grams (g).

Record your estimate here: _____ g

Have three people in your group use a balance to measure the mass of the pencil in grams. Don't peek at each other's measurements; just record whatever each person gets.

_____ g   _____ g   _____ g

Step 3: How much liquid does a glass hold?

Your teacher will give you a beaker or **graduated cylinder** for this activity.

Estimate the volume of the glass in milliliters (ml).

Record your estimate here: _____ ml

Have three people in your group use a graduated cylinder or measuring beaker to measure the volume of the glass. Don't peek at each other's measurements; just record whatever each person gets.

_____ ml   _____ ml   _____ ml

Think It Over

1. Were all three measurements of height, mass, and volume the same? Why do you think this is?

   _____

   _____

   _____

2. If you had to pick one measurement from the three as the best measurement in each case, which would you pick? Why?

   _____

   _____

   _____

3. Estimates are usually not the same as the measured amount. How close were your estimates to what you measured? Subtract the middle values of the amounts that you measured from the values of your estimated amounts.

   estimated height − measured height = _____

   estimated mass − measured mass = _____

   estimated volume − measured volume = _____

4. Making estimations can be tricky because your eyes can sometimes play tricks on you. Look at these figures and answer the questions without measuring. Then check your answers by measuring.

   Which is longer: the top of figure A or the top of figure B?

   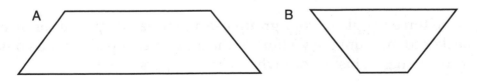

   Which is longer: line segment *a* or line segment *b*?

   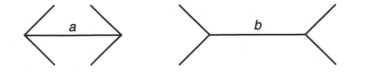

Is the top hat taller than the brim is wide, or is the brim wider than the hat is tall?

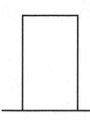

Practice Questions

1. Miles and Graham are running a scientific investigation to find out whether their new freezer can freeze water more quickly than their old one. Which of the following would be the least useful item of data that they could collect?

    A. the temperature in the new freezer

    B. the height and weight of the new freezer

    C. the amount of water placed in each freezer

    D. the time it took to freeze a cup of water in the old freezer

Directions: Mariano is testing the living conditions of his goldfish, Blinky. Use this information to answer Numbers 2 and 3.

2. Which instrument should Mariano use to find out whether the depth of the water in the fish tank is the same each day?

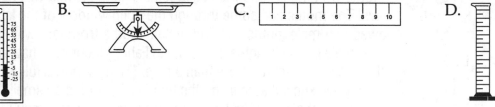

3. Mariano feeds Blinky every day. Which instrument should Mariano use to find out how much the food weighs?

4. Three fourth graders want to find out which of their bicycles is the fastest at coasting down a hill. Which of the following scientific instruments would provide the most useful data?

A. meterstick and stopwatch

B. telescope and camera

C. microscope and balance

D. barometer and thermometer

5. What is the best way to make sure a measurement is accurate?

A. Make a good estimate.

B. Have someone else measure for you.

C. Take the measurement several different times.

D. Compare your guess with your measurement.

People in Science

The Great Peacock moth has wings five or six inches wide. One morning, a female peacock moth hatched in Jean-Henri Fabre's home laboratory. He put her in a cage made of gauze and forgot about her. That night, Fabre heard thumping and yelling from his son's bedroom. Paul Fabre had been getting ready for bed when some giant moths flew into his room. Father and son ran to the laboratory. There, they saw male moths whirling around the caged female like bats in a wizard's cave. The moths had come through the open window of the lab. They showed that male moths can find female moths from far away. Some of the male peacock moths that came to Fabre's laboratory had followed the female's scent for more than a mile. (That's a powerful perfume!) Today, we know that male moths find female moths by smell. Female moth scent also can be used to trap pests, such as gypsy moths.

Jean-Henri Fabre
(France 1823–1915)

Review 4

Recording and Reporting Results

Have you ever heard the expression "A picture is worth a thousand words"? A graph is a way of representing numbers in picture form. Graphs and tables make it easier to interpret a lot of numbers. They can help you communicate data from a scientific investigation. Scientists also use graphs and tables to record and communicate their evidence from experiments. Graphs and tables also help scientists to see patterns and find results that differ from other results. Sometimes, these different results point them to new, interesting findings. This review will give you practice in organizing and interpreting evidence in graphs and tables.

What Do You Think?

Your teacher will tell you how many students are in each grade in your school.

Write down the number of students in each grade in the table that follows.

Grade	Number of Students

Do you see any patterns in your data? What are they?

_____

_____

_____

_____

Key Words

bar graph

circle graph

conclusion

evidence

journal

line graph

map

table

Now create a graph in the space below that shows, in picture form, how many students are in each grade in your school.

Now, based on the numbers in the table and the graph that you created, write one question that could be the start of a new investigation.

_____

_____

_____

What People Think

While collecting data, it is important that you understand what you see, form a **conclusion**, and share the results. This last step is very important: Scientists always ask themselves and other scientists, "How do you know that?" or "How does your **evidence** support your conclusion?" Sharing information is the only way to be sure.

Recording the results of an experiment is the first step toward communicating them to the rest of the world. Scientists look at changes in the natural world. Scientists describe these changes by recording the conditions before *and* after the experiment. Then they compare the two sets of information and describe the change. In this way, the work of scientists builds on itself. Scientists check the accuracy of each other's work, and they use that work to develop and conduct new experiments.

How does keeping records during a scientific investigation help scientists study the changes that occur in the natural world?

_____

_____

_____

When scientists interpret data, they look for patterns. Making graphs and tables makes those patterns easier to see. Graphs and tables are both mathematical models: They use numbers to create a model of the actual event. This is helpful in a number of ways. First, as you learned in the last review, using math to communicate helps make sure that anyone in the world can understand the results of your experiment, no matter what language they speak. Plus, math lets us keep close track of changes in the natural world. For example, Ginny wants to track how fast her fern plant grows. Without measuring and keeping records, she might have a hard time tracking the changes.

On Wednesday, Ginny's fern plant is 190 mm tall. On Friday, it is 198 mm. In the space below, write out a mathematical equation that describes the growth of the fern plant during that time.

Additionally, graphs and tables make it easier to spot information that is somehow different from the rest of the data. This difference could be an error in measurement or it could be an interesting new event that should be studied. As you record the results of your investigations, keep your eyes out for strange-looking data.

Graphs come in three main types: bar graphs, circle graphs, and line graphs.

A **bar graph** can be used to compare data that can be put into separate groups. Imagine you have collected data about the different ways students travel to school in the morning. A bar graph like the one to the right can be a good way to compare the groups of data in this kind of research.

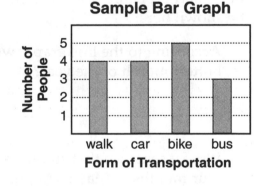

Sample Bar Graph

According to the sample bar graph, how many people take the bus?

_____

Write a sentence that summarizes and describes the general information contained in the bar graph.

_____

_____

_____

A **circle graph** is used when you want to show the parts of a whole. If you wanted to show what percent of students in your class (a whole) has brown eyes (a part), you would probably use a circle graph as shown here. Circle graphs are also called *pie charts*.

Sample Circle Graph

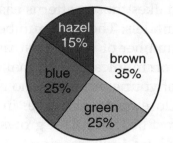

How many different eye colors are represented in the circle graph?

_____

Write a sentence that summarizes the information presented by the circle graph.

_____

_____

_____

A **line graph** shows how data change over time. If you were going to graph the average high temperatures in a city for a certain period of time, you would probably use a line graph such as the one shown here.

Sample Line Graph

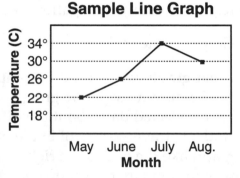

According to the line graph, which is the hottest month of the year?

_____

Write a sentence that summarizes the general pattern of temperature for the four months of May to August.

_____

_____

_____

Scientists use surveys to find out what people think. Surveys are one way to gather data. Another way, which you studied in Review 3, is observing. Scientists cannot ask plants, animals, or rocks what they think, so they observe them and gather data that way. Many types of observations take place over long periods of time, often many years. Scientists record their data in **journals** so they can look at changes that take place over time.

Why do you think scientists write down what they see?

_____

_____

_____

In science and many other areas, people use **tables** to organize their data. Tables make it easier to understand data. Tables use rows, which run side to side, and columns, which run up and down. Each box within a table is called a *cell*. To understand a table, look at the title (if there is one) and the first row (often called the *column headers*). These will usually tell you exactly what the table is about.

For example, look at the table to the right. The title and the column headers (the shaded boxes) tell you that this table compares time and temperature of water being heated. You can use the columns and rows to find what you are looking for. For example, suppose that you wanted to find the temperature of water at 180 seconds. First, find 180 seconds in the *Time* column, and then find the *Temperature* cell that is in the same row. The temperature of the water at 180 seconds was about 11° Celsius. Tables also make it easier to see patterns. This table shows a clear pattern: As time passes, temperature goes up.

Heating Water

Time (seconds)	Temperature (C)
0	1°
60	3°
120	8°
180	11°
240	14°
300	17°

How long did the water have to heat to reach 14° Celsius?

_____

Ricardo recorded the amount of rainfall over a seven-day period as follows: "Sunday (2 mm), Monday (17 mm), Tuesday (0 mm), Wednesday (1 mm), Thursday (25 mm), Friday (2 mm), Saturday (0 mm)."

Arrange Ricardo's data in the following table. Be sure to add a table title and column headers.

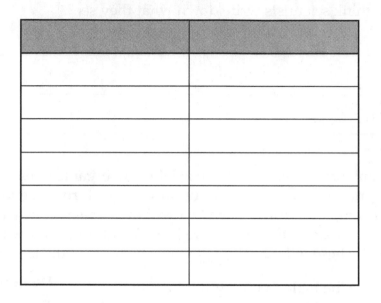

Another great way to present information is with a **map**. Maps represent an area on the Earth, in the sky, or even on another planet. Maps can represent small areas: Your classroom might have a small map of your school showing the quickest way to exit in case of fire. Maps can also show gigantic areas: Astronomers use maps to find stars in the sky. Maps can show you how close things are to each other, and they can tell you a lot about the features of a certain place. The map on page 39 shows the average yearly precipitation (rain, snow, or any other form of water) for New York.

Average Annual Precipitation in New York

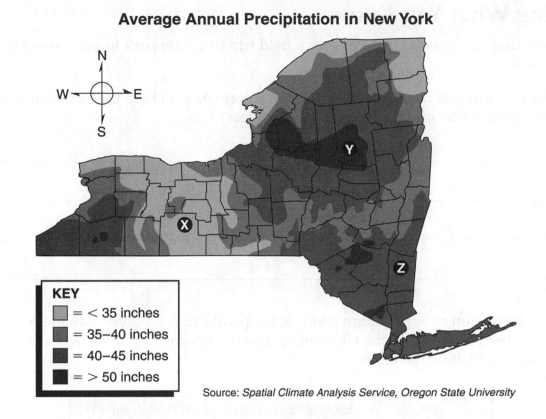

KEY
☐ = < 35 inches
▨ = 35–40 inches
▩ = 40–45 inches
■ = > 50 inches

Source: *Spatial Climate Analysis Service, Oregon State University*

Which area experiences the highest average amount of precipitation: X, Y, or Z?

_____

What is the average annual precipitation for the area in which you live?

_____

Like every model, graphs, tables, and maps do not represent their subjects perfectly. All models have limitations, which means that they leave out parts of the story so they can describe one part more clearly. Because of this, scientists include written reports of their studies that help explain their findings. Throughout this workbook, and in the rest of your scientific studies, you will be asked to share your findings with others. Scientists know that sharing information helps scientific research continue. Other scientists who learn about the new information might come up with ideas that extend knowledge in new directions.

Using What You Know

Pretend that you are making plans for a field trip to a state park in your area a year from now.

How could you use this year's weather information to help predict what kinds of clothing you might need to wear next year?

_____

_____

_____

_____

Some information about the high and low temperatures for a given day in six U.S. cities has been gathered in the table below. Use the information to answer the questions that follow the table.

City	High Temperature (F)	Low Temperature (F)
Buffalo, NY	79°	57°
Rochester, NY	83°	62°
Brooklyn, NY	82°	60°
Madison, WI	76°	58°
Denver, CO	79°	59°
Seattle, WA	64°	53°

Which temperatures were most likely recorded in the daytime? Why do you think so?

_____

_____

Based on this assumption, which city had the warmest temperature reading during the daytime?

_____

Which city had the warmest temperature at night?

_____

Do you think these temperatures were recorded in the summer or winter? Why do you think so?

_____

_____

What would you predict the high and low temperatures to be in Manhattan, New York, on the day the data in this table were collected? What information did you use to make your predictions?

_____

_____

Think It Over

Mr. James's fourth-grade class was learning about the weather. To help their studies, they created their own school weather station. Two students, Mary and Chris, were assigned to read and write down the temperature each day. The readings they took are shown in the table below. Each student read the thermometer and wrote down the temperature reading at three different times during the day.

Temperatures (F)

Day of the Week	Mary's Data			Chris's Data		
	8 A.M.	noon	3 P.M.	8 A.M.	noon	3 P.M.
Monday	70°	82°	90°	69°	82°	91°
Tuesday	52°	65°	75°	52°	66°	76°
Wednesday	64°	72°	75°	64°	72°	76°
Thursday	71°	80°	85°	71°	80°	86°
Friday	72°	82°	90°	32°	81°	91°

1. What was Mary's temperature reading for Tuesday at noon?

_____

2. What was Chris's temperature reading for Tuesday at noon?

_____

3. Even when Mary and Chris read the same thermometer at the same time, their readings were a little different. How would you explain the difference?

_____

_____

_____

4. When you look at the patterns in the numbers that Mary and Chris wrote down, in which set of data do you see a number that looks like a possible mistake? Why do you think this number may be wrong?

_____

_____

_____

5. When you compare Tuesday's temperatures with Monday's temperatures, what do you think the weather might have been like Monday night?

_____

Support your idea about Monday night's weather, using evidence from the table to write a logical conclusion.

_____

_____

_____

_____

_____

Practice Questions

Directions: Use the following paragraph and graphs to answer Numbers 1 through 3.

Susie and Bridget were preparing a project for their science class. They collected weather data for one week. However, the class took a field trip on March 15, and the girls were unable to record any weather data except the sky conditions because they were away from their equipment. To share their information, Susie and Bridget made the following two graphs.

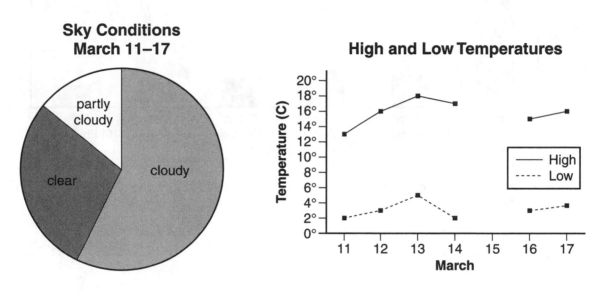

1. Which sentence best describes the pattern of temperatures Susie and Bridget measured?

    A. Temperatures got colder through the week.

    B. When highs got warmer, lows got colder.

    C. When highs got warmer, lows got warmer.

    D. The difference between highs and lows showed no pattern.

2. If the girls had been able to record the temperatures on March 15, which of the following would they most likely have recorded?

    A. high 4° C, low 4° C   C. high 30° C, low 0° C

    B. high 16° C, low 2° C   D. high 13° C, low 10° C

3. Which of the following conclusions can be made based on the evidence in the circle graph?

    A. Rain fell on more than half of the days.

    B. The skies were cloudy more than half of the days.

    C. The Sun shone for some of each day during the week.

    D. The "partly cloudy" days were more cloudy than clear.

Directions: Use the following graph to answer Numbers 4 and 5.

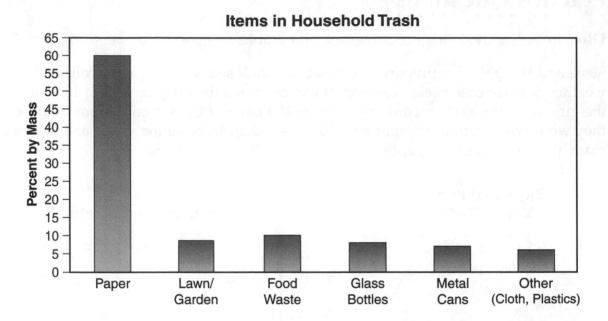

4. Using the graph, predict which of the following would be found most often in household trash.

   A. soup cans

   B. grass clippings

   C. newspapers

   D. leftover food

5. Which information about household trash cannot be determined from the graph?

   A. the total number of tons of food waste found in it each year

   B. the different kinds of items usually found in a typical landfill

   C. whether glass bottles or metal cans make up a larger percentage of trash

   D. which type of trash item is probably most abundant in the nation's landfills

Review 5

Science, Technology, and Society

Every day, you use and rely on many technologies. For example, you probably eat fresh fruits and vegetables that come from other states or faraway countries. Moving fruits and vegetables long distances and keeping them fresh requires much **technology**. This review is about technology—the problems it solves and the problems it causes.

What Do You Think?

Blaise went to the movies with some friends last Saturday. They saw *The Savage Robots of Zendor*, which was about these robots who turned against their human inventors and tried to take over the galaxy. Blaise loved the movie, but he was a little concerned about the robots.

Could something that humans invented turn against us?

_____

Can you think of some technological problems in your town? How about in the state of New York?

_____

_____

_____

What People Think

We use scientific knowledge to create technology to use in our everyday lives. Technology affects the way people live and act. Humans usually create new technology to solve a problem or make life more enjoyable. For example, dishwashers save much time and effort, and satellites make it possible for people to get information very quickly and from far away.

What are at least two things we need to know from science in order to make satellites that orbit the Earth and send weather information, TV signals, or photographs to us?

_____

_____

Key Words

cost-benefit analysis

hardware

simulation

society

software

technology

In our **society**, many people view science and technology as the solution to all our problems. However, there are also many people who think that the more we rely on computers, machinery, and chemicals, the worse off we'll be in the future. Both sides have a point: Every technology has both positive and negative effects, and it is almost impossible to see *all* the negative effects of a technology before we put it to use. The important thing is to learn as much as we can about the science behind technologies so that we can make better decisions about them. We are all members of society, which means that we are all connected to one another. Because we are connected through society, everyone, not just scientists, should stay aware of the benefits and costs of all technologies.

Cost-benefit analyses (plural for *analysis*) are good tools for measuring how a new technology will affect society and the environment. Although it sounds like a difficult thing, a cost-benefit analysis is simply listing all the negative effects that a technology might have, then listing all the positive effects, and then comparing the two lists. Does the good outweigh the bad? Is there a way to get rid of some items on the bad list? For example, nuclear power plants provide an inexpensive, plentiful energy source. But they also present serious risks of dangerous accidents and extremely harmful pollution.

Any time you balance the positive effects of a decision against any negative side effects you can think of, you perform a cost-benefit analysis. Sounds important, doesn't it? You use this type of thinking any time you plan on buying a product. Let's look at an example.

> Reggie really wants a new pair of Athena™ basketball sneakers. They're really comfortable and look great. Lots of other kids have them. They cost more than $100. Reggie's dad thinks that they are made out of cheap materials. List the costs and benefits on the lines below.

Costs: _____

_____

Benefits: _____

_____

Think about farming for a moment. More than 6 billion people live in the world today, and we all need to eat. We have developed fertilizers to grow more crops in smaller areas. Fungicides protect plants from the fungi that can kill entire crops. Chemical pesticides control the insects, weeds, and small mammals that can ruin crops. However, all these chemicals can cause water pollution in the surrounding areas and beyond. They can also cause disease in humans. Some people believe that these harmful chemicals show up in the foods we eat.

What are some ways that farmers could reduce the negative effects of these chemicals?

_____

_____

_____

_____

Another example of technology that has greatly changed the world is the automobile. It used to be much more difficult to travel long distances than it is now.

What problems have been solved and caused by the use of cars and trucks?

Problems that have been solved: _____

_____

_____

Problems that have been caused: _____

_____

_____

One technology that has become important in recent years is the personal computer. Computers are great tools for making sense of data. They also help scientists communicate the results of their research. Let's take a look at how computers help us process and communicate scientific data.

Any computer is made up of two systems: hardware and software. **Hardware** is all the equipment needed to run the computer. This includes the keyboard, the mouse, the monitor, the circuit boards, the disks, and all the chips used to store and process information. **Software** is the set of instructions (the program) that tell the hardware what to do. There are software programs that tell a computer how to turn on and off, let you play your favorite games, help run businesses, and allow scientists to control robots on other planets. To compare hardware and software, think about how you are reading this workbook. The book itself, your eyes, and your brain are the hardware: the equipment that stores and processes the information. The ideas and meanings of the words are the software: the message of the system.

Right now, you are holding a pen or pencil and getting ready to answer the following question: Is the pen or pencil an example of hardware or software? Why?

_____

_____

_____

_____

Scientists often use computers to help them run their experiments and then analyze and present their data. Many classrooms use computers in their science laboratories, as well. **Simulations** are extremely important software programs for scientific investigations. They use the calculating power of a computer to recreate events that are too dangerous, expensive, or time-consuming to produce in a regular laboratory. For example, you might use a computer simulation to study how much pollution a typical coal-burning power plant produces. The simulation provides you with good data and lets you avoid having actual coal burning in your classroom! Still, simulations cannot replace actual experiments, which provide the best data.

Here are some other important jobs that computers do. Some of these you already do, but others might be unfamiliar to you.

- Word processing: Before computers, scientists used to write out their reports by hand or type them on a typewriter. Word processors allow the user to make changes, rearrange sentences, and even insert graphs and pictures.

- Database: This is an electronic storage system that can hold huge amounts of data. It also organizes "raw" data so that humans can make sense of it. Databases are often stored on servers, powerful computers that many people can use at one time.

- Graphing: Some programs automatically change numbers into graphs and tables. These programs can help you create clear, attractive graphs that communicate your data well.

- Information technology: One of the greatest technological achievements of the past 30 years has been the connection of millions of people through electronic communication. The Internet, the World Wide Web, and other networks allow users to find enormous amounts of information. Many scientists communicate with each other only on the Internet.

Imagine you are a scientist working with *Cassini,* a robotic spacecraft that is collecting data from the planet Saturn and its moons. *Cassini* is sending huge amounts of raw data back to Earth. Right now, the data do not make sense to humans.

What type of computer system will help you store and organize all this information?

_____

Using What You Know

Your teacher will divide you into five groups and give each group a newspaper. The newspaper may be from your local town or city, or it may be from another part of New York. Look through the paper with your group and find three articles that address a technology issue. Read them out loud to each other, and discuss what the positive and negative sides of the technology might be. One important point before you begin: Many articles that don't look like they're about technology will still have some important technological issues that you could discuss!

1. Article title: _____

   Technology issue: _____

   _____

   Positives: _____

   _____

   Negatives: _____

   _____

2. Article title: _____

   Technology issue: _____

   _____

   Positives: _____

   _____

   Negatives: _____

   _____

3. Article title: _____

Technology issue: _____

_____

Positives: _____

_____

Negatives: _____

_____

Think It Over

1. After discussing your findings with your class, what do you think is the most important technological issue facing your town or city?

_____

_____

2. Describe two ways you could learn more about this issue.

_____

_____

3. What do you think is the most important technological issue facing the state of New York?

_____

_____

4. Describe two ways you could learn more about this issue.

_____

_____

_____

Practice Questions

1. Which of the following is the best description of how a new technology affects human life?
   A. It always does good for humans.
   B. It always ends up doing harm to the environment.
   C. It has many bad effects, which we always know about in advance.
   D. It has both good and bad effects, but we can't always predict what those are.

2. Which of the following is an important advance in the technology of nutrition?
   A. the invention of the automobile
   B. the discovery of vitamins
   C. the invention of the microwave
   D. the discovery of electricity

3. Humans often change their environment without meaning to damage it. Even so, damage sometimes happens. This damage is often caused by which of the following?
   A. bad weather that changes the environment
   B. poor planning for cold winters and hot summers
   C. not thinking about what might happen to the environment
   D. people making mistakes in completing the changes

4. What type of computer technology allows students to view a "virtual" volcanic eruption without leaving their classroom?
   A. database
   B. simulation
   C. word processor
   D. graphing program

5. If your town decided to build a new park, how might it affect the environment?
   List at least three ways building the park might affect the environment.

_____

_____

_____

_____

_____

People in Science

When he was 19, William Perkin was a chemistry research assistant in London. His job was to find a use for coal tar—a black, gooey material left over when coal is made into fuel. One thing found in coal tar is aniline. Aniline is similar to quinine, the medicine used to cure malaria. Because there was a shortage of quinine in England, Perkin decided to try changing the aniline in coal tar into quinine. He tried some different mixtures. To his surprise, one mixture turned mauve, a shade of purple. He had invented a new kind of dye. Perkin's father used his life savings to set up a small dye factory. Soon, the new color was everywhere. Even Queen Victoria wore clothes colored with Perkin's dye. Although Perkin never made quinine from coal tar, his dye made him wealthy enough to retire when he was 36 years old.

William Perkin
(England 1838–1907)

Review 6

Designing Technology

Do you like to make sand castles? Lots of people do. In fact, you probably know some adults who turn into little kids again when they start digging around in the sand. Many engineers began their careers thinking about the problems of building sturdy sand castles. Before you begin a sand castle, you decide whether to make it a tall, pretty structure or a tough building that will survive some ocean waves. This process of identifying the important features of an engineering design is the same, whether you're building sand castles or a real building. In this review, you will learn how to identify an engineering problem. You will also complete an engineering design of your own.

What Do You Think?

When you build a sand castle, you are making a model of a real castle. In some ways, you face the same problems that a medieval engineer had to face.

What are some important design features of a real castle?

_____

_____

_____

_____

Why were large stones used so much in castles?

_____

_____

_____

_____

Key Words

brainstorming web

constraint

design

engineer

graphic organizer

prototype

What People Think

Whether we're building castles or designing frost-free refrigerators, we use scientific knowledge to create technology that we use in our everyday lives. Technology can be described as **design**, the process of putting ideas to work. Technologists are constantly trying to invent or develop something to help people solve their problems.

Engineers identify problems in our lives, and they think of solutions to those problems. When new technology is created, it is usually because someone wanted to solve a problem or make life easier. For example, automobiles were invented to allow people to get places more quickly.

For each of the inventions below, identify the human need that led to its development.

Paper towels: _____

Ceramic roof tiles: _____

Indoor plumbing: _____

Ice makers: _____

Technological designs are usually improvements on prior solutions to problems. For example, people used wood shingles, straw, or other materials to cover their roofs before ceramic tiles. Whenever you are faced with a technological problem, you should look into the problem and find out how people tried to solve it in the past. Look at books, magazines, and the Internet. Ask your friends, family, and teachers for information. These sources can all help you find your own improvements to existing solutions.

Here are some activities that people have needed help with. For each problem, identify a technology that has been invented to solve it. Then suggest one improvement to the existing technology.

Problem	Technology	Improvements?
Mending torn clothing		
Cutting down trees		
Eating food		
Heating food		
Holding clothing closed		

When engineers begin to design a technological solution to a problem, they must decide what is the most important feature of the design. This process involves figuring out the **constraints** of a design. Constraints are all the things that keep a design from being perfect—and no design is ever perfect. For example, a bridge designer knows that the most important feature of the bridge will be strength and stability. However, there are constraints: The strongest available materials may be too heavy or expensive to use. When you design the features of your own engineering solutions, you will also have to work under some constraints.

Paco wants to design a high-speed train that will carry more than 1,000 passengers. What are the most important design features for the train?

_____

_____

What are some constraints that Paco needs to consider?

_____

_____

Technology and engineering designs sometimes seem very futuristic. However, engineers often look to nature to help them model their ideas. Many engineering designs try to copy an existing natural shape or structure. For example, early boatbuilders used the shape of a fish to improve their designs. Sometimes, however, designs must be different from the natural version. For example, the Wright brothers designed a successful airplane by making wings that were rigid. Previous airplane designers had failed because they tried to copy the flapping of a bird's wing.

Why wouldn't a wing modeled on a bird's wing work for an airplane?

_____

_____

_____

To summarize, creating the most effective engineering design requires that you define the engineering problem and then identify the most important features of its solution. You can also look to the natural world for inspiration. A good way to get started is to brainstorm and communicate your ideas to others. Sometimes, when you are stuck on a part of the problem, it helps to have your partners check out the ideas you have so far. There are a lot of useful ways to share your early ideas.

Imagine you are in charge of designing a new form of transportation for you and your friends. In the space below, use a sketch, a diagram, or a list to describe the engineering problem.

Engineers often use **graphic organizers** to develop their ideas. A graphic organizer is a mixture of sketches, diagrams, and lists. A **brainstorming web** is a type of graphic organizer. With it, you start by writing down the most important part of the problem and circling it. Then, in another circle, you write another part of the problem, or you can include possible solutions. As you add more and more circles, you connect them with lines or arrows. If you want, you can label the lines or arrows to describe how the two circles relate to each other.

The following is a brainstorming web used by an engineer to get started on an idea for a lightweight train that runs between her house and her school.

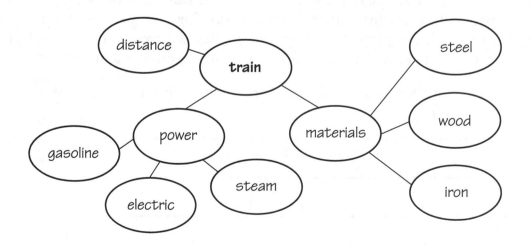

In the space below, create a brainstorming web to develop your ideas for your new transportation system.

Once you've decided on the initial idea, determined what the right materials are, and brainstormed all the possible problems and solutions you can, it's time to build a **prototype**, the first construction of a new idea. Working things out on paper is important, but many problems can only be fixed by building a prototype. Prototypes are full-sized versions of an idea, but they are rough, which means that they are not meant to be the completed idea. You've heard the phrase "back to the drawing board," right? Well, engineers don't get upset when they hear that. In fact, they're *looking* for problems during the prototype tests. Engineers know that the best way to come up with a good design is to test a prototype, find its faults, and then go back to the drawing board to design the thing all over again. After many cycles of this, they are ready to construct the final version.

As with your scientific investigations, the best way to keep track of changes in your designs is by using mathematics. For example, imagine you are designing a paper airplane that can fly in a long, straight line. You have made your first prototype. After you run the first test, you should measure how far the plane flew. Using that number, you can compare the later throws to the first throw. You can track how each new design changes the distance flown. For example:

Design 1: flew 59 cm

Design 2: flew 72 cm

Difference: The second plane traveled 13 cm farther than the first. Our design is on the right track.

The more complicated the design is, the more important it is to record measurements in mathematical form. Also, using math to describe your results will allow you to put them into graphs and tables, as you learned in Review 4.

As you design technological solutions of your own, keep the following ideas in mind:

- Define the problem clearly. Sometimes technologies don't work out because the designers didn't really know what the problem was: The design may have been good, but it solved the wrong problem. Always take the time to ask a lot of questions about the problem before beginning a design project.

- Choose the best materials for your design. Again, the best approach here is to ask a lot of questions, such as "Will wood bend enough for this job?", "Does my design need to be fireproof?", and so on.

- Stay flexible during the construction process. As you build your design, think about different ways of putting it together. If one of the new ways makes sense, try it out.

- Test, test, and retest. Try out your design as many times as necessary before you call it finished. Often, a design will work really well once but fail every time after that. Make sure that your design stands up to repeated tests.

Using What You Know

Using only the materials that your teacher provides, design a prototype structure that will protect an egg from being broken when it is dropped at least 3 meters.

Step 1: Use a separate piece of paper or a notebook to create a journal for this activity. In your journal, sketch out a brainstorming web to explore solutions, materials, and any problems you expect to face in this project.

Step 2: Now design a prototype structure that will protect your egg. In your journal, sketch the prototype you have designed.

Step 3: Explain how your prototype will protect the egg from breaking.

_____

_____

_____

_____

Step 4: Build and test your prototype. In your journal, keep notes on the test process.

Step 5: Present your prototype, testing process, and results to your classmates.

Think It Over

1. What sorts of tools helped you accomplish your task?

   _____

   _____

   _____

2. What part of your prototype worked best in protecting the egg? How did it help?

   _____

   _____

   _____

3. What part of your prototype didn't work very well in protecting the egg? Why do you think it didn't work very well?

   _____

   _____

   _____

4. If you were able to repeat this process, how would you improve on your prototype?

   _____

   _____

   _____

Practice Questions

1. Scott and Zelda have entered a kite-building contest together. What are the two most important design features they should look for when selecting the material for building their kite?
   A. length and cost
   B. weight and strength
   C. shape and color
   D. texture and flexibility

2. What is the best way to test whether an egg carton protects eggs against damage in a grocery cart?
   A. Drop the carton with eggs inside.
   B. Drop the carton without eggs inside.
   C. Stack things on top of the carton with eggs inside.
   D. Stack things on top of the carton without eggs inside.

3. What is the purpose of designing a prototype?
   A. to test a design idea on a full-scale level
   B. to build the final version of a design idea
   C. to create a miniature model of a design idea
   D. to make multiple copies of the finished design

4. Think back to the prototype structures you and your classmates designed to protect a dropped egg. How were the best egg protectors alike?

   _____

   _____

   _____

5. It is often said that "necessity is the mother of invention." What does this mean?

   _____

   _____

   _____

   _____

UNIT 2

Earth and Space Science

Review 7

Solar System Cycles

As you read this page, the Earth is spinning around at about 1,600 km/hr (1,000 mph) at the equator, and it is **orbiting** the Sun at 107,000 km/hr (67,000 mph). Can you feel it moving at these great speeds? What clues do you have that the Earth is moving at all? It's not easy to think about all this motion. One idea that might help is that all this motion happens in cycles. Cycles are repeating patterns, and humans have learned to predict these patterns. The cycles of the solar system are so predictable, in fact, that we base our days, months, hours, and other units of time on them. In this review, you'll learn about some of the patterns in the movements of the Sun, Earth, and Moon. You will also see how the seasons on Earth are caused by these movements.

What Do You Think?

If you are like a lot of other people, you look forward to the arrival of summer. You also may know that summertime in North America is wintertime in South America.

What do you think causes the **seasons** on the Earth?

_____

_____

_____

Key Words

apparent motion

axis

eclipse

gravity

orbit

phase

revolution

rotation

seasons

solar system

time

Why don't North and South America have summer at the same time?

_____

_____

In the box below, draw a diagram that shows the Earth, the Moon, and the Sun. Use lines and arrows to show how they revolve around each other.

What People Think

The Sun is a medium-sized yellow star. It is one of billions of stars in our galaxy. Some giant stars are many times larger, hotter, and brighter than the Sun—some so large, in fact, that their outer layers would extend past Jupiter if they were in the place of our Sun! Other stars are even smaller than the Earth, and still others do not give off much heat or light at all. All of the stars in the night sky are very far away. If you could travel at the speed of light (the fastest we think anything can go), it would still take you nearly 5 years to reach the closest star.

The Sun is the central anchor for the **solar system**. The Sun contains about 99% of the mass of the entire solar system. It is made up mostly of hydrogen and helium gases; the hydrogen reacts constantly to create a kind of nuclear furnace. These reactions produce the heat and light that the Sun gives off. The Sun's **gravity** works on the planets, holding the moving system together. Earth is one of nine planets in the solar system, the third closest to the Sun. Earth's Moon is one of many moons in the solar system.

The Earth moves through space in predictable and repeating patterns. Humans have used their knowledge of these patterns to create a system for keeping **time**. As you may recall, the Earth rotates (spins) around an **axis**, an imaginary pole going through the Earth from the North Pole to the South Pole. If you can imagine the Earth as a giant basketball spinning on someone's fingertip, then you have a good idea of the Earth's **rotation** on its axis. We define a day, then, as the amount of time it takes the Earth to complete one rotation—to spin around once. A week is defined as 7 days. If one rotation (1 day) is sliced up into equal parts, we find all the units of time shorter than a day. Look closely at the following diagram.

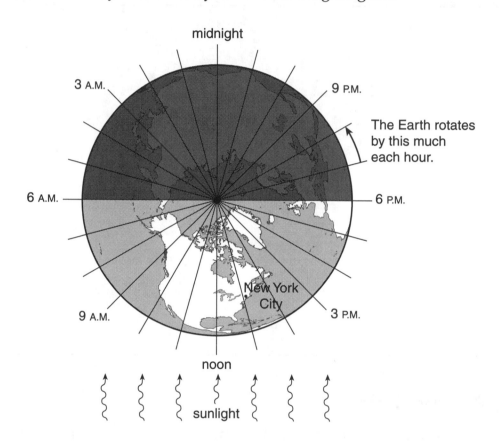

In this view, we are looking down at the North Pole from outer space, and the Earth rotates counterclockwise. The Earth's rotation has been sliced up into 24 equal parts. An hour is the amount of time it takes for the Earth to rotate the distance of one of these 24 slices. There are 24 hours in 1 day. If you took one of the "hour slices" and cut it into 60 equal parts, that would give you the distance the Earth rotates in 1 minute. Slice up one of the "minute slices" into 60 equal parts, and you'd get 1 second, far too small to see on this map.

Using the 24-hour map above, what time is it in New York City? Try to estimate to the closest minute.

How long will it be until sunset in New York City?

_____

Longer periods of time shown in a calendar—months and years—are not defined by the Earth's rotations but by the Earth's revolutions. A **revolution** is the movement of the Earth in its orbit around the Sun. We define 1 year as the amount of time needed for the Earth to complete one trip around the Sun, a revolution. As the diagram below shows, one revolution (1 year) is divided into 12 parts to give each of the 12 months.

One Revolution, Twelve Months

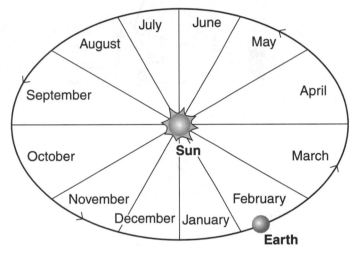

Even though this system of keeping time is the best one that humans have developed so far, it still has a few small problems. For example, the Earth rotates 365.25 times each time it completes one revolution. In other words, after every year there is an extra 0.25 days to deal with. In 4 years, that adds up to a whole day. So every 4 years, we add a "leap" day to the end of February to eat up that extra day. The years 2008, 2012, 2016, and so on will have 366 days instead of 365.

The Moon also follows regular patterns as it rotates and revolves around the Earth. These patterns are so regular and predictable that humans used to base the calendar on the Moon before we knew about the Earth's movements. The Moon takes about 28 days to complete one revolution around the Earth, and a month used to be exactly 28 days. (The word *month,* in fact, comes from the word *Moon.*)

Revolution and Phases of the Moon

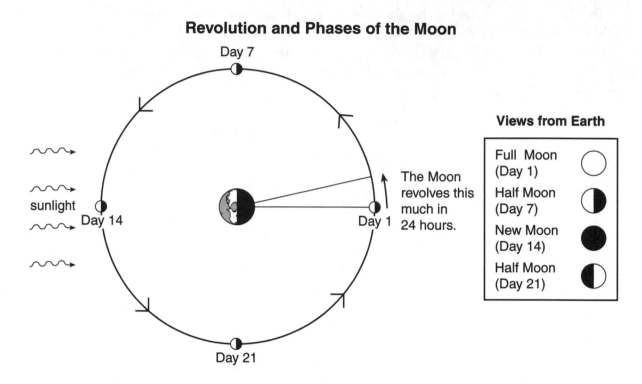

The Moon's monthly revolution around the Earth causes different parts of the Moon's surface to be lit up by the Sun. From the Earth, we see different shapes of the Moon, called **phases**. Some people incorrectly use the term "dark side of the Moon" to refer to the side of the Moon that is always pointed away from the Earth. However, it is not always dark: Each time the Moon rotates on its axis, the far side of the Moon gets a lunar day of sunlight. A lunar **eclipse** occurs when the Earth casts its shadow on the Moon. A solar eclipse happens when the Moon casts its shadow on the Earth; from our view on Earth, the Moon blocks out the Sun.

Write a sentence that describes why the appearance of the Moon changes over the course of one month.

_____

_____

_____

The Earth is slightly tilted as it goes around the Sun. This is the cause of the seasons. The places that receive the most direct sunlight heat up the most. As the illustrations below demonstrate, the Northern Hemisphere's summer happens when it is tilted toward the Sun (*left*); at the same time, it is winter in the Southern Hemisphere because the Southern Hemisphere is tilted away from the Sun. Six months later, the Southern Hemisphere is tilted toward the Sun (*right*) and has summer, while the Northern Hemisphere tilts away for its winter.

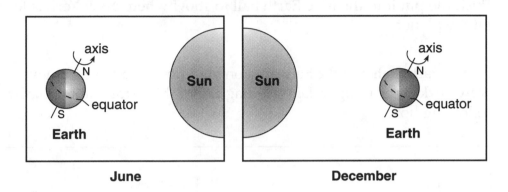

Think about how you answered the questions earlier about the cause of the seasons. Do you want to change your answers? If so, how?

_____

_____

_____

The Earth's rotation and revolution make it look like the Sun and the other stars are moving around us, but this is an illusion. Astronomers refer to this as **apparent motion.** The rotation and revolution of Earth cause apparent motion in the stars and other objects in the night skies. These objects don't really move around Earth in one day: Our *view* of them changes gradually throughout the night—and quite a lot from season to season—as we turn and move through space. Astronomers can predict the apparent motions of the Sun, the Moon, the planets, the stars, and many other objects.

Using What You Know

Now that you know about the motions of the Earth, Moon, and Sun, it's time to create a model illustrating the phases of the Moon. For this activity, you will need a pin, a large blue ball to represent the Earth, a small white ball to represent the Moon, and a lamp to represent the Sun. You may work in groups of four.

Step 1: Push the pin into the blue Earth ball to show where New York is located on the planet.

Step 2: Set the Earth ball and the Sun lamp on your desk or a table to show New York state at night. Draw a diagram of this arrangement in the following box.

Step 3: Using the Earth ball and Sun lamp, demonstrate and describe the Earth's orbit as it revolves around the Sun.

_____

_____

_____

Step 4: Using the large ball and the small ball, demonstrate and describe the motion of the Moon orbiting the Earth.

_____

_____

_____

Step 5: Demonstrate how a full moon occurs. Illustrate your results in the space below.

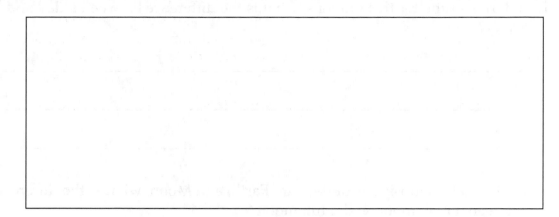

Step 6: A new moon occurs when the Moon is not visible in the sky at night. Arrange your Earth, Moon, and Sun to demonstrate how a new moon occurs every month. Illustrate your results.

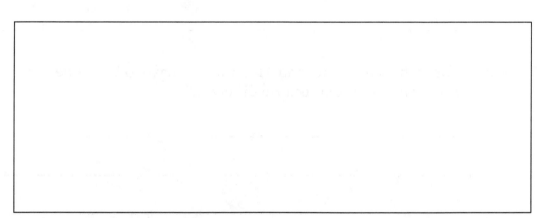

Think It Over

1. In terms of the Earth's motions, what is the difference between a day and a year?

   _____

   _____

   _____

2. Looking at the positions of the Sun, Earth, and Moon, what is the difference between a new moon and a full moon?

   _____

   _____

   _____

3. Describe how the Sun, Earth, and Moon would have to be aligned to create a lunar eclipse. How is a solar eclipse different?

   _____

   _____

   _____

4. When we see the Moon, light is being reflected off the Moon's surface. Where does this light come from?

   _____

   _____

Practice Questions

Directions: Use the following diagram to answer Numbers 1 and 2.

The Moon orbits the Earth in a little more than 27 days, for a total of 13 times per year. The Earth orbits the Sun in a little more than 365 days, for a total of once per year. The Moon travels along with the Earth in an orbit around the Sun.

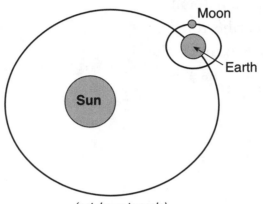

(not drawn to scale)

1. About how many times does the Moon circle the Sun each year?

   A. 1

   B. 13

   C. 27

   D. 365

2. During a solar eclipse (when our view of the Sun is blocked), what happens to block our view of the Sun?

   A. The Earth's shadow falls on the Sun.

   B. The Moon's shadow falls on the Sun.

   C. The Moon passes directly between the Earth and the Sun.

   D. The Earth passes directly between the Moon and the Sun.

3. The Sun is at the center of our solar system. Which of the following is another word for our Sun?

   A. star

   B. planet

   C. galaxy

   D. meteorite

4. Which of the following is the best description of one week on Earth?

   A. 1 revolution of the Earth

   B. 7 rotations of the Earth

   C. 7 revolutions of the Moon

   D. 28 rotations of the Moon

5. The seasons on the Earth are determined by what?

   A. the Moon's gravitational pull

   B. the speed of the Earth's rotation

   C. the Earth's distance from the Sun

   D. the tilt of the Earth on its axis

People in Science

As a young girl in Germany, Caroline Herschel was very bright and loved music. But when she was 10, typhus stunted her growth, and her parents did not believe she would ever marry. So at age 23, she went to live with her older brother William, who was a professor of music in England. There she was a professional singer and studied mathematics and astronomy as well. William also became something of an expert in astronomy and wanted Caroline to assist him in his research. Caroline gave up her music to help her brother. After William discovered the planet Uranus, the king asked him to be Great Britain's Royal Astronomer; the king later hired Caroline, too. She became the first woman to discover a comet (in all, she discovered eight comets), and she discovered 14 nebulae (collections of gas and dust in space). She was awarded several gold medals in science, and, to this day, no one has ever found an error in her mathematical calculations. Finally, when she was 78 years old, Caroline was able to return to her first love, music. To her surprise, the great violin player Paganini wanted to meet her—Caroline Herschel, the famous lady astronomer!

Caroline Herschel
(Germany 1750–1848)

Review 8

Weather and the Water Cycle

What is **weather**? You might think that weather is only the sky conditions at any given moment: sunny, cloudy, or something in between. But weather is much more complicated than that. It involves the Earth's oceans, its landmasses, the blanket of air called the atmosphere, and even the Sun. As you read in Review 1, scientists make models to help them understand how complex systems work. This review will focus on how one such model—the water cycle—helps explain why the weather does what it does. You will also learn how to describe the weather, keep records of it, and study the weather patterns in the United States.

Key Words

aquifer	groundwater	runoff
atmosphere	humidity	water cycle
condense	meteorologist	water vapor
evaporate	precipitation	weather
forecast		

What Do You Think?

You might know that a **meteorologist** is a scientist who studies the atmosphere and the weather. Of course, you can always find information about the weather by looking outside. But if you want to measure weather conditions and predict what they will be like in the future, you need to have some tools.

Using your own knowledge or a dictionary, write down what weather condition is measured by each of the following tools.

Thermometer: _____

Anemometer: _____

Barometer: _____

What People Think

To understand how water moves through the Earth system, it is important to understand the **atmosphere**, the blanket of air that surrounds the Earth. The atmosphere is very thin compared to the rest of the Earth, but it still contains an enormous amount of gas, water vapor, and solid material such as dust. The atmosphere is also constantly moving. Imagine yourself standing on the bottom of an ocean of air and you'll get the idea. Currents and streams of air move throughout the atmosphere. You can feel some of these as wind. You can see the effects of currents high up when you see clouds moving quickly across the sky.

When air moves, it usually carries some water with it. The **water cycle** explains how water travels between places that are not connected by direct waterways. For example, the water cycle explains how water gets from the oceans to Lake Erie or a landlocked lake high up in the Rocky Mountains.

The water cycle moves water from the ocean to the land and back to the ocean again. Water in the ocean heats up and **evaporates**, or turns into water vapor. The **water vapor**, or gas, rises into the atmosphere and is moved by the wind. The cooler temperatures high in the atmosphere cause the water vapor to **condense** back into tiny droplets of liquid and form clouds. Eventually, the water falls to the ground again as **precipitation**. The temperature of the air around the clouds determines the kind of precipitation that falls. If it is very cold at the level of the clouds, snow will fall; if it is warmer, the precipitation will be rain.

Water from precipitation has two places to go: It can either run off the land or soak into it. Most water ends up as **runoff**. Runoff water goes into lakes and rivers. Most of it eventually ends up in the oceans. Water that soaks into the Earth is called **groundwater**. This water can collect in underground layers of rock, gravel, or sand to form **aquifers**. New York has many such aquifers, and these provide a great deal of freshwater for drinking, industry, and agriculture.

Add labels to the following illustration of the water cycle. Use these terms: *condensation*, *evaporation*, *precipitation*, *runoff*, *water*, and *water vapor*.

We use the word *weather* to describe the combined conditions of the atmosphere at any specific time. These conditions include air temperature, wind speed and direction, precipitation, and cloud cover. Many factors affect weather conditions, including the way that the Sun's energy hits the Earth, the water cycle, the rotation of the Earth, and the behavior of the air.

When would someone say, "There is no weather today"? Why is this an incorrect statement?

_____

_____

_____

In which direction do most weather systems travel in New York?

_____

_____

_____

If you set a cold glass of water in hot sunlight, you'll see that drops of water form on the outside of the glass. This isn't because the glass has holes that allow water to leak through! These drops are condensation. The cold temperature of the glass has caused water vapor (gas) in the air to condense, or form into drops of liquid water, on the outside of the glass.

You probably also know that if you leave a glass of water sitting out for some time, the water in the glass will disappear. Where does it go? The process of evaporation causes the liquid water to turn into water vapor and rise into the air. Meteorologists measure **humidity**, which is the amount of water vapor in the air.

As you read earlier, water moves between the oceans, air, and land through the water cycle. The water cycle drives the Earth's weather. The energy that causes the water cycle comes from the Sun. The Sun warms the land and the water on the Earth so that the water evaporates and moves into the sky. Once the water vapor cools, it forms clouds. Eventually, the water from the clouds falls back to the Earth as precipitation, and the cycle starts over again.

List as many types of precipitation as you can.

_____

_____

_____

Probably the easiest weather-watching job is to describe the cloud cover (sky conditions). There are five general levels of cloud cover. It isn't realistic to measure exactly how much of the sky is covered, so these terms and percents are used as estimates.

Cloud Cover

Term	Approximate Cloud Coverage
Sunny (or Clear)	0%
Mostly Sunny (or Mostly Clear)	25%
Partly Cloudy (or Partly Sunny)	50%
Mostly Cloudy	75%
Cloudy	100%

Describe the cloud cover in your area at this moment.

_____

By learning to identify the four basic cloud shapes, you can start predicting the weather yourself.

Cirrus: The highest clouds, cirrus look like feathers of ice running across the sky. They are found around 10,000 meters above the Earth. Cirrus clouds usually bring fair weather.

Cumulus: These clouds look like bright white wads of cotton in the sky. Cumulus clouds form at about 6,000 meters above the Earth. Cumulus clouds are most often seen with fair weather.

Cumulonimbus: The largest clouds, cumulonimbus look like gigantic anvils: wide at the bottom, narrowing in the middle, then wide and flat at the top. They begin at about 2,000 meters, but they pile upwards to as high as 9,000 meters. Cumulonimbus clouds bring heavy rain, high winds, hail, and tornadoes.

Stratus: These clouds form gray sheets that spread across the sky. They form at around 1,500 meters, and they can sink all the way to the ground. Stratus clouds often bring heavy mist and snow or drizzle.

Some days, it might seem like the air isn't moving at all. Actually, the air never stops moving, even though it might seem still to us. Air is matter, just as water or rock is. There can be more air in one place than another. Differences in temperature and in the amount of air in two places cause wind. How does this work? Well, imagine a balloon filled with air. There is more air packed into the balloon than right outside it. If you open the balloon, the air rushes out. Wind works in the same way. Because the Earth is such a gigantic place, wind never stops moving and is quite powerful.

Wind speed is usually described in miles per hour. (Meteorology is one of the only areas of science that uses inches, miles, and so on instead of the metric system.) Wind direction is described by the direction from which the wind blows. For example, a north wind comes from the north, a west wind come from the west, and so on. On weather maps, wind direction and speed are shown using symbols such as the following:

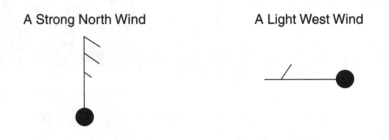

The tail of the symbol, like the feathers on an arrow, points to where the wind is coming from. The dot points to the direction the wind is going. The barbs on the tail show the speed of the wind: The more barbs there are, the faster the wind is going.

Clouds, winds, and precipitation are only part of what meteorologists study. They study many other features of the weather, too. All over the world, people collect data about the weather. This information is fed into computers and recorded on maps and charts. Then meteorologists study what is happening and use their knowledge to **forecast** the weather to come.

Changes in the atmosphere can produce some dramatic, violent weather. These severe weather systems can cause enormous damage, so it is important to be aware of their causes and effects.

Tornado: These small storms produce the strongest winds on Earth, sometimes topping 300 miles per hour. Tornadoes form when hot, moist air rises quickly to meet cool, dry air above, forming the familiar funnel cloud. These twisters can create paths of destruction that stretch for dozens of miles.

Thunderstorm: When warm, moist air rises and cools quickly, thunderstorms can occur. These large storms produce violent winds, heavy rain, and lightning. Lightning is unpredictable and dangerous, so you should wait at least 30 minutes after a thunderstorm has passed before going outside.

Blizzard: When cold, northern air bulges south and meets with warmer, southern air, blizzards can result. These winter storms have high winds, very cold temperatures, and heavy snow. Blowing snow reduces visibility, making it impossible to see farther than several meters.

Hurricane: These severe tropical storms form over warm sections of the ocean. If conditions are right, a huge storm forms that rotates in a counterclockwise direction. Hurricanes usually have a calm spot in their center called the *eye*. Winds outside the eye are at least 74 miles per hour. Most of the hurricanes that affect the United States form in the Atlantic Ocean.

Using What You Know

Much weather is caused by the unequal heating of land and ocean water. In this investigation, you will observe differences in how quickly soil and water absorb and release heat.

Your teacher will provide you with one cup filled with soil, another cup filled with salt water, a heat lamp, and two thermometers.

Step 1: Place a thermometer in the center of each cup. Record the starting temperature.

Step 2: Place both cups under a heat lamp (or bright lightbulb) for 5 minutes.

Step 3: Take temperature readings every minute during the 5 minutes. Record your results in the table below.

Step 4: Turn the heat lamp (or bright lightbulb) off and record the temperature every minute for another 5 minutes.

Heating Time (minutes)	Temperature (C)		Cooling Time (minutes)	Temperature (C)	
	Soil	Salt Water		Soil	Salt Water
0			0		
1			1		
2			2		
3			3		
4			4		
5			5		

Think It Over

1. How did the temperature readings of the soil and salt water compare during heating and cooling?

   _____

   _____

   _____

2. In general, if an object absorbs a lot of energy but heats up slowly, that object takes a long time to release the energy it has absorbed. How does this statement relate to the data collected from your investigation?

   _____

   _____

   _____

3. If you're at the beach in the middle of July when the temperature outside has been very hot, your feet can nearly burn on the sand and yet feel chilly when you put them in the water. Explain why this happens.

   _____

   _____

   _____

Practice Questions

1. Mountain climbers need to bring containers of air to breathe when climbing tall mountains. Why is this?

    A. The climbers are going high up in the Earth's atmosphere, so the air is too thick to breathe.

    B. The climbers are going high up in the Earth's atmosphere, so the air is too thin to breathe.

    C. As the climbers get close to the Sun, the air becomes too warm to breathe.

    D. The climbers get close to the Moon, which steals away Earth's atmosphere.

2. Which of the following is not a feature of the weather?

    A. the kind of clouds

    B. the speed of the wind

    C. the position of the stars

    D. the temperature of the air

3. A person in Simon City reports a temperature of 35° C, the same temperature that another person in Hecklertown observes. But clothes on a clothesline in Simon City are taking longer to dry than clothes on a clothesline in Hecklertown. What is the likely explanation for this occurrence?

    A. The air is more humid in Simon City.

    B. The air is not as warm in Simon City.

    C. The air is more humid in Hecklertown.

    D. The ground is much warmer in Hecklertown.

4. Which process causes water vapor to form?

    A. Clouds cool and form precipitation.

    B. There is too much water in the atmosphere.

    C. Water on the ground or in the ocean heats up.

    D. Water runs over the land and picks up pollutants.

5. The water cycle involves evaporation and condensation. Which of the following do evaporation and condensation cause together?

    A. erosion

    B. pollution

    C. the seasons

    D. precipitation

Directions: Use the following information to answer Number 6. The weather symbols in the box are used to show wind strength on a weather map.

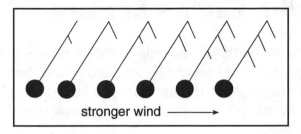

stronger wind ⟶

Flags X and Y are in two different cities. The wind symbol for the city of Flag X is shown below the flagpole.

Flag X   Flag Y

?

6. What wind symbol would be used for the city where Flag Y is located?

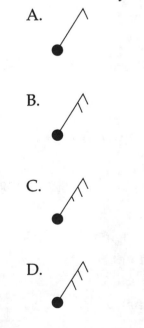

A.

B.

C.

D.

Changes to the Earth's Surface

If you could speed up time so that hundreds of thousands of years could be squeezed into a few seconds, you would be amazed at the dramatic changes that occur on the Earth's surface. Most of these changes take a very long time, but some happen fairly quickly. In this review, you will examine some of the processes that change the Earth's surface.

What Do You Think?

The surface of the Earth is constantly changing. Sometimes the changes occur very slowly. In fact, some changes occur so slowly that you would have to live many, many thousands of years to notice even a small difference. In other instances, the changes occur very quickly. The places where fast changes happen on the Earth's surface can be very dangerous places to live, as shown in the photograph below.

Key Words

erosion

glacier

humus

ice wedging

sediment

volcano

weathering

In the following table, identify some things that cause rapid changes on the Earth's surface. Then identify some things that cause slow changes on the Earth's surface.

Causes of Fast Changes on the Earth's Surface	Causes of Slow Changes on the Earth's Surface

What People Think

Many decades ago, when farmers wanted to remove a very large rock from their land, they would wait until the time of year when the nights were very cold and the days were warm. When that time of year arrived, they would pour water into the cracks of the rock during the day. The next morning, they would often find that the cracks had become larger or that the rock had split entirely into pieces. The farmers would repeat this process day after day until the pieces were small enough to carry off.

What property of water were the farmers using to break such large rocks into smaller ones?

_____

_____

_____

Sediments are very small pieces that break off rocks. Rocks and other materials are broken down by natural forces through the process of **weathering**. Causes of weathering include wind, water, and living things. The freezing and cracking that occur in rocks are a type of weathering called **ice wedging**. This is what the farmers you read about earlier were doing. You may have noticed an example of ice wedging after the snow melts in the springtime: During winter, water gets into cracks in the street, and as it freezes, it expands and cracks the pavement. This same process occurs in natural rock, as well.

When sediment is moved to another place by wind, liquid water, ice, or gravity, the process is called **erosion**. **Glaciers** are gigantic formations of ice that do not completely melt over a year. These giant ice formations can quickly erode rock, grinding mountains into valleys and carving out lakes. Glaciers once covered much of North America, and you can still see evidence of them in the lakes, mountains, valleys, and ridges of New York. Rivers, too, erode and shape landscapes in often dramatic ways. The Colorado River carved the Grand Canyon out of the gigantic plateau of northern Arizona. The Mississippi deposits sediment where it enters the Gulf of Mexico—so much that the land is extending outward into the sea.

Give an example of a natural formation that results from erosion.

_____

_____

Wind, water, and glaciers can move sediments many miles away from their original rocks. Soils are made partly from the sediments weathered from rocks. Because of this, a single area might have many different types of soils—some made from nearby rocks, others made from distant materials.

Holly studied some soil at the bottom of a valley. The soil contained some rock particles from the top of a nearby mountain. Explain how the particles could become part of the soil.

_____

_____

_____

The weathering of rock is only the first step in making soil. It takes nonliving and living things to make soil. As plants and animals die, their remains mix with the rock material to form humus. **Humus** is dark brown or black, and it is the basis for a healthy, rich soil. Plants and animals release materials that make the soil richer. Also, worms and other, smaller living things move through the soil, breaking apart lumps and mixing the soil.

What makes up the nonliving part of soil?

_____

What part of soil comes from living things?

_____

It takes about 100,000 years for fully developed soil to form. Fully developed soils have several layers. Each layer holds a different type of soil. The closer the soil is to the bedrock, the more pebbles and rocks there will be in the soil. The top layer is called *topsoil*, and it is the best type of soil for growing plants because it contains the most humus.

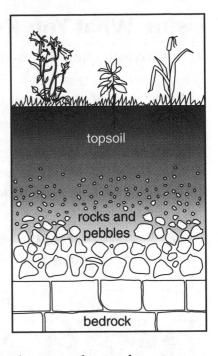

Scientists and farmers can learn a lot about a soil by studying its properties. For example, a soil's color and texture provide information on the types and sizes of the materials it holds.

Weathering, erosion, and soil formation all take many years to affect a landscape noticeably. Some changes to the Earth's surface, however, happen much more quickly. Far beneath the Earth's surface, temperatures are so high that rock turns to liquid. This liquid moves around in huge currents, which sometimes cause changes here on the surface. **Volcanoes** are found at hotspots in the Earth's crust, places where the liquid rock pushes up through the solid rock. The materials that erupt out of volcanoes provide clues about what is deep within the Earth.

How might the eruption of a volcano give scientists clues about the materials deep within the Earth?

_____

_____

_____

_____

_____

Using What You Know

In this investigation, you will be testing the effects of vinegar (acetic acid) on rocks.

Step 1: Your teacher will give you six beakers, three containing 100 ml of distilled water and three containing 100 ml of white vinegar.

Step 2: Collect two fragments of each of these three types of rocks: granite, limestone, and sandstone.

Step 3: Place each of the rock fragments into the appropriate beaker according to the tables below.

Distilled Water Observations

Rock Type	0 minutes	5 minutes	10 minutes
Granite			
Limestone			
Sandstone			

Vinegar Observations

Rock Type	0 minutes	5 minutes	10 minutes
Granite			
Limestone			
Sandstone			

Step 4: Leave the rocks in the beakers for 10 minutes. Record your observations directly after placing the rocks into the beakers (0 minutes), after half the testing time (5 minutes), and at the end of the testing time (10 minutes).

Think It Over

1. In which beaker did you observe the strongest reaction?

   _____

   _____

   _____

2. How can you tell if a chemical reaction is taking place?

   _____

   _____

   _____

3. Predict what would happen to the rocks in each of the beakers if you were to leave them in the solution for 10 years.

   _____

   _____

   _____

   _____

Practice Questions

1. Over very long periods of time, mountain ranges are slowly worn down by all of the following except which?

   A. gravity

   B. erosion

   C. weathering

   D. volcanoes

2. What material do sand, silt, and clay combine with to create soil?

   A. humus

   B. topsoil

   C. pebbles

   D. earthworms

3. How many years does it take for a fully developed soil to form?

   A. 10

   B. 150

   C. 1,000

   D. 100,000

4. Which of the following geologic processes is the most difficult to see actually happening?

   A. a landslide

   B. mountain building

   C. a volcanic eruption

   D. erosion caused by wind

5. Using examples from this review, describe the difference between weathering and erosion.

   _____

   _____

   _____

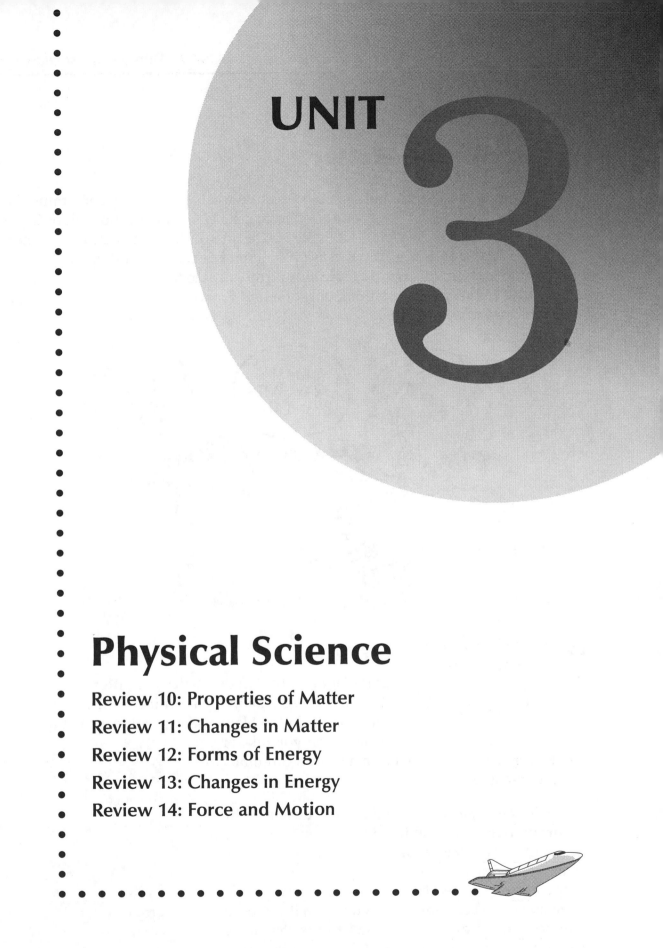

UNIT 3

Physical Science

Review 10

Properties of Matter

I Spy is a fun game. People find an object that they can see and say something like "I spy something green." Everyone else has to ask yes-or-no questions in order to try to guess what the object is. Is it living? If the answer is *no*, this means it is not a frog or the leaves on a tree. You can ask if it is rigid or flexible, soft or scratchy, solid, liquid, or gas. As you get more clues, you are able to figure out what the object is. Scientists follow a similar question-and-answer process when figuring out the basic properties of matter.

What Do You Think?

Have you ever thought about the number of different types of **matter** you interact with on a daily basis? From the time you get up in the morning until you go to bed at night, you use matter and rely on it. Cotton blankets keep you warm at night. Plastic helmets protect your head when you bike or skateboard. Different kinds of matter can do some wonderful things.

Just as in the *I Spy* game, we describe substances by the **properties** they exhibit. Suppose you were trying to describe water. How might you describe it? Some of its properties are that it is a **liquid** (at room temperature), it's clear and colorless, it flows, it takes the shape of its container, it has no odor, it can become **solid** ice when frozen, and it can become steam, the **gas** form of water, when heated. We are able to use water for certain tasks because of its properties.

Key Words

conduct

gas

liquid

mass

matter

property

solid

volume

List some substances that you regularly work with in the table below. Describe as many properties of those substances as possible in the second column. Two substances have been listed to get you started.

Substance	Properties
Copper penny	Shiny, conducts electricity, conducts heat, solid, hard, copper colored, smooth
Cotton balls	White, fluffy, soft, can be pulled apart into strands

What People Think

We interact with substances all the time. Most of the time, however, we don't think about the objects we interact with; we simply use them. In this section, you will start to think about how to describe different kinds of materials and why we use certain materials for certain jobs.

There are lots of ways to describe objects. In the space below, describe a warm chocolate chip cookie as fully as you can. What does it feel like, smell like, and look like?

_____

_____

_____

Think about a building. In the space below describe the building. What is it made from? What does it look like? What does it smell like and feel like?

_____

_____

_____

You're probably familiar enough with chocolate chip cookies to think of quite a few ways to describe them. But how do we classify matter that is not as familiar—or that is too small to be seen by the human eye? Scientists have developed ways to describe the properties of all sorts of substances, from the most common element to the rarest metal.

Matter has volume and mass—two properties that we can measure. **Mass** is the amount of matter in something, and **volume** is how much space something takes up. There are other properties of matter that we can measure as well. We can find out the temperature of an object. We can also describe an object by how it looks: Is it a solid, a liquid, or a gas? Is it smooth or bumpy? Is it bendable or rigid? Is it shiny or dull?

Some features of an object change depending on the environment. For example, a glass of water that has a temperature of 35° C has that temperature because the water was either heated or cooled to that temperature. Water isn't always 35° C. Similarly, objects can appear different if they are wet or if the light changes. The object still has the same properties, but its environment has changed.

Think back to your description of a building. A building's materials must be hard and sturdy, so it is obvious why buildings are made of steel, glass, concrete, brick, stone, and wood instead of water, cotton, or cardboard. A building usually has electricity and plumbing. The pipes that carry water or the wires that **conduct** electricity must be made of special materials. For example, you wouldn't make your pipes out of cardboard. If you did, they would quickly leak and fall apart. Plastic or metal pipes work better because they are waterproof. The building must have wires that conduct electricity, or nothing electrical would work.

Name a feature of a building not already mentioned. What is it made of? What are the important properties of that material that make it good for its purpose?

_____

_____

_____

Some materials are useful to human technology because they conduct electricity, heat, or light. Metals are some of the best conductors of heat and electricity. Special plastic or glass cables are used to conduct light. Circuit testers are tools that measure how well a material will conduct electricity.

Name a material that is a good conductor of heat. How might humans use this material? Does it conduct electricity as well?

_____

_____

_____

_____

Scientists have to do more than understand and describe the properties of substances. They must also understand how to take correct measurements.

Imagine that you have a solid block of ice, and you need to measure its temperature, volume, and mass. What tools could you use to accomplish this task?

_____

_____

_____

As mentioned earlier, mass represents the amount of matter that makes up an object, and it is usually measured in grams (g) or kilograms (kg). As mass increases, the number of particles increases. Mass can be measured using a balance.

The tools for measuring the properties of matter depend on what state that matter is in. Imagine that the block of ice you wrote about earlier suddenly melted. You could still use a thermometer for temperature and a scale or balance for mass. However, you could not use a ruler to measure volume—the amount of space a substance occupies—because liquid water does not have length, width, or height on its own. Rather, a liquid will change shape to fit whatever container it is in. When we measure the volume of liquids, we use a graduated cylinder. These are much like the measuring cups that you might have in your kitchen at home, only more accurate and precise. A graduated cylinder measures volume in liters (l) or milliliters (ml). Cubic centimeters (cm^3) are also used to measure volume ($1 \ cm^3 = 1 \ ml$).

Using What You Know

Your teacher is going to give you a collection of items. Your task is to come up with several different ways of grouping the items. Record your answers on a separate piece of paper.

Step 1: Sort the items into groups based on how they appear (color, shape, size, shine). Record which items are in each group.

Step 2: Sort the items into groups based on how they feel (smooth, rough, bumpy, scratchy). Record which items are in each group.

Step 3: Sort the items into groups based on how they act with a magnet. Record which items are in each group.

Step 4: Sort the items into groups based on what they do when dropped into a cup of water. Record which items are in each group.

Step 5: Sort the items into your own groups and label them with the property used. Record which items are in each group.

Think It Over

1. Which material would be best to use if you were going to make a bed? Why do you think so?

    _____

    _____

    _____

2. Which material would be best to use if you were building a car? Why do you think so?

    _____

    _____

    _____

3. Which material would be best for building a boat? Why do you think so?

_____

_____

_____

4. Which material would be best for making a pot for cooking? Why do you think so?

_____

_____

_____

Practice Questions

Directions: Use this chart to answer Numbers 1 and 2.

Mineral	Luster (shiny or dull)	Hardness similar to	Color
A	shiny	penny	transparent
B	dull	fingernail	black
C	shiny	steel file	white
D	dull	steel file	transparent
E	dull	window glass	black
F	shiny	window glass	white

1. What property or properties could be used to group minerals A and C together?

   A. color

   B. luster

   C. hardness

   D. color and luster

2. What property or properties could be used to group minerals B and E together?

   A. hardness only

   B. luster and color

   C. hardness and color

   D. luster and hardness

3. Look at the following groups of objects. Which properties could have been used to sort them?

Group 1

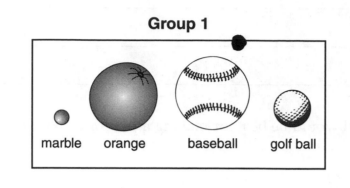

marble   orange   baseball   golf ball

Group 2

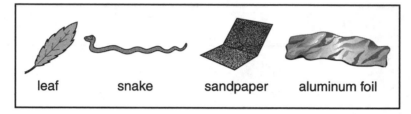

leaf   snake   sandpaper   aluminum foil

   A. solid colored vs. multicolored
   B. living vs. nonliving
   C. round vs. nonround
   D. magnetic vs. nonmagnetic

4. Suppose you wanted to make a container to hold hot soup in your lunch bag. The container (like a thermos) has to keep your soup hot for several hours. Which of the following would be least important to you?
   A. The container should be magnetic.
   B. The container should be lightweight.
   C. The container should be waterproof.
   D. The container should keep heat trapped inside.

Review 11

Changes in Matter

Felipe and his younger sister Mira were enjoying popsicles outside on a hot July afternoon. Mira carefully put her half-eaten popsicle back in its wrapper, set it on the steps, and went inside to get a glass of water. When she came back, the popsicle was gone.

"Where did my popsicle go?" she asked Felipe.

"It changed states," replied her brother, and he licked the last green, sugary drops off his popsicle stick.

Mira wasn't sure what her brother was talking about: How could the popsicle get up and walk to New Hampshire? But then she noticed the pool of green liquid on the step below her wrapper. As you learned in Review 10, one property of matter is its **state**—whether it is solid, liquid, or gas. In this review, you will learn what happens when matter moves from one state to another. And don't worry: You won't have to leave New York to find out.

What Do You Think?

Think about putting some ice cubes in a glass of water on the kitchen counter and in a bowl of water in the microwave. After a few minutes, the ice in the glass **melts**, and the water in the bowl reaches the **boiling** point.

What happens to the ice when it melts?

_____

What happens to the water in the glass after the
ice cubes are added?

_____

_____

What happens to the bowl of water when
it boils?

_____

_____

Key Words

boil

condense

freeze

melt

mixture

physical change

state

water vapor

What People Think

Most people know that water will **freeze** (turn to ice) when it is left outside on a cold winter night. In addition, ice will melt if it is left out in a room where it is not so cold. What people might not realize is that water and ice are the same kind of matter. When water freezes or ice melts, a form of water has changed states. No, it hasn't moved from New York to Iowa, but rather from solid to liquid or liquid to solid. Water can also change from liquid to gas or gas to liquid; other possible changes are from solid to gas or gas to solid.

Water is certainly not the only substance that can change states. Almost every other kind of matter can exist in solid, liquid, or gaseous states. However, most kinds of matter—except for water—need extreme temperatures, hot or cold, to change states.

The three main states of matter are as follows:

- solid, in which matter has a definite shape and volume
- liquid, in which matter has a definite volume but no definite shape
- gas, in which matter has neither a definite shape nor a definite volume

A change in states is a type of **physical change**. A substance that has gone through a physical change has not become a new kind of matter. Some of its physical properties have changed, but it is still the same thing it was. For example, solid water has a certain mass, volume, and shape. Liquid water has a certain mass and volume, but its shape can change to match its container. Gaseous water has a certain mass, but its volume can expand, and its shape will change to fill its container. Even though its physical properties change from state to state, the substance is still water.

It is important to remember that physical changes are reversible. Ice that melts to water can freeze back into ice. Gas that condenses to liquid can boil back into gas. If a substance has been changed so that it *cannot* be changed back, then it did not go through a physical change.

The table below is partially completed with the general properties of solids, liquids, and gases. Complete the missing parts of the table.

State of Matter	Mass	Volume	Shape
Solid	doesn't change	doesn't change	
Liquid	doesn't change		changes
Gas		expands to fill container	

Even a penny, which is made of zinc and copper, will change to a liquid state if it is heated to a high temperature. As long as it stays very hot, the metal will be in a liquid state. When it cools off, it will change back to a solid state.

Are chocolate chips and melted chocolate the same kind of matter? What makes them different from each other?

_____

_____

What happens to water that is placed on a hot stove? It boils away and seems to disappear into thin air. Is this really what happens? Actually, in a way, this is exactly what happens. When water is heated up enough, it changes into a gas that we call **water vapor**. It is still water, and it hasn't really disappeared, but it is now a part of the air around you.

When water in the air changes back to a liquid, we say it **condenses**. Outdoors, water that comes back out of the air can do so in a lot of different ways. Rain occurs when water condenses in a cloud and then falls.

What are some other ways that water can condense outdoors?

_____

_____

If you left a pot of water on a hot stove in a closed room, what would happen to the water?

_____

_____

A **mixture** combines two or more materials without changing their properties. Because a mixture is the result of a physical change, it can be reversed. Many mixtures will keep some properties of the materials that go into them. Consider a mixture of lemon juice, sugar, and water: lemonade. The water brings the property of being a liquid, which is a good thing if you like to drink lemonade instead of chew it. The sugar makes the mixture sweet, and the lemon juice makes it tangy. Because it is a mixture, the lemonade can be separated into its ingredients.

Think of another mixture. Describe how its ingredients affect the mixture's properties.

_____

_____

_____

_____

Using What You Know

Step 1: Your teacher will give you an ice cube. Squeeze the ice cube in your hand for about 10 seconds. (Hold it over a paper towel.)

What happens to the ice cube? To your hand?

_____

_____

_____

If you were thirsty in the winter, could you "drink" snow? Why or why not?

_____

_____

_____

Step 2: Walk over to a window. Put your face as close to the window as you can without touching it. Open your mouth wide and blow gently on the window.

What forms on the window?

_____

Where did it come from?

_____

_____

Think It Over

1. Ice melting into water or water freezing into ice are examples of a physical change in matter. What are some other examples of physical changes?

_____

_____

_____

2. Jason claims that a candle is just frozen wax. Why might he think this? Do you agree with him? Why or why not?

_____

_____

_____

3. How would you explain to someone what happens to matter when it changes states?

_____

_____

_____

Practice Questions

1. When water freezes into ice, which of the following is true?

    A. The ice has a smaller mass than the water.

    B. The ice has a greater mass than the water.

    C. The ice has a lower temperature than the water.

    D. The ice has a higher temperature than the water.

2. What could you do to show that ice melting into water is a physical change?

    A. Melt more ice to see if it also becomes water.

    B. Take the water outside to see if it condenses.

    C. Put the water into a freezer to see if it refreezes.

    D. Put the water into a pan on a hot stove to see if it boils.

3. Simon left a glass of ice water on the table. When he returned a few minutes later, there were beads of water all over the outside of the glass. What happened?

    A. Ice formed on the outside of the glass and then melted.

    B. Water vapor from the air condensed on the cooler glass.

    C. Tiny droplets of water were able to leak through the glass.

    D. Water vapor rose from the ice water and then dripped down the sides of the glass.

4. A goldsmith melts a small amount of gold to make a ring. Which of the following statements about the state of the gold is true?

    A. Most of the gold disappears as a gas when it melts.

    B. Gold can be melted and cooled to a solid countless times.

    C. It isn't gold anymore, since the liquid can't change back into a solid.

    D. The process of condensation will bring the gold back to a solid form.

5. A chef wants to make her sauce even tastier, so she boils it a little longer. What does she accomplish by doing this?

    A. The gases in the sauce are changed to liquids.

    B. Extra heat energy causes some of the ingredients to condense.

    C. The boiling causes a physical change that increases the amount of sauce.

    D. The sauce thickens as some of the water turns into vapor and disappears into the air.

Review 12

Forms of Energy

Have you ever been on a swing and wondered what you could do to swing higher? Are there ways you could swing faster? Swinging and other kinds of motion involve energy. Energy exists in several forms, such as chemical, potential, heat, kinetic, electric, light, and sound. After you complete this review, you just might be able to swing better than anyone else in your neighborhood.

What Do You Think?

Pretend your school is going to have a "Science Olympics," and you're on the rope swing team. Your job is to set up two swings and choose the riders. You have to make sure that one swing rider will swing out and back in exactly 1 second. The other swing rider must swing out and back in exactly 3 seconds.

Key Words

chemical energy	kinetic energy	open circuit
closed circuit	light	pendulum
conductor	luminous	potential energy
electricity	magnetism	reflection
energy	mechanical energy	solar energy
heat energy	medium	sound
insulator		

You need to design the two rope swings for your team. What do you know about how and why things swing that will help your team win?

_____

_____

_____

_____

What People Think

Many people think that the weight at the end of the swing is the only thing that matters in figuring out how quickly it will swing back and forth. After all, it is harder to push an adult on a swing than a child. But, in fact, the swing rider's weight does not affect how long it takes to go back and forth. The thing that matters most is the length of the swing.

What is one way you could test to see if weight on a swing affects how much time it takes for the swing to go back and forth?

_____

_____

_____

_____

_____

Understanding swings requires understanding **energy**, which is the ability to cause change or make things move. **Mechanical energy** is energy that can cause objects to move. There are two types of mechanical energy: Energy of position is called **potential energy**, and energy of motion is called **kinetic energy**. What do these terms mean? To get started, think about a **pendulum**, which is an object such as a rope swing that can swing freely. It takes energy to lift up the weight on the end of a pendulum (sometimes called a *bob*). When the pendulum bob is pulled back and lifted up, it has potential energy. This means that it has the ability to do work or to move because of its position and Earth's gravity. The higher it is lifted, the more potential energy it has.

If you let go of the pendulum bob, it will swing back down. As it swings down, its speed increases. Kinetic energy results from the mass and the speed of the moving object. The pendulum bob starts out with all potential energy at the top of its swing. At the bottom of its swing, it has all kinetic energy.

It takes energy to lift a hammer. What kind of energy does a hammer have when it is held high above a nail?

_____

What kind of energy does the hammer have right before it hits a nail?

_____

Everything in the universe is either matter or energy. Matter is the "stuff" of the universe; everything that has mass is made of matter. You can see energy (light), feel it (heat), and hear it (sound), but it doesn't exist in the same way that matter does. Think of matter as the "nouns" of the universe and energy as the "verbs," the forces that make everything go. We can see how energy affects matter all the time. For example, **chemical energy** is stored in the food we eat, and we use it to keep our bodies running. When a car engine burns gasoline, it uses the chemical energy in the gasoline to move the engine. As you will learn in Review 13, energy can be changed from one form to another. We see this every day, as electricity is converted to light in lightbulbs. Let's take a quick look at some of the most important types of energy.

mirrors

Light is one of the most important forms of energy. Without it, we wouldn't be able to see the objects around us, and plants wouldn't grow. Although light doesn't look as if it has any color, it is actually made up of all the colors that you see in a rainbow. Light comes from many different sources. When something produces light, we say it is **luminous**. We see most other things—such as the Moon or a glowing movie screen—because of the **reflection** of light. These objects reflect light waves from other sources; in other words, light waves bounce off these things and travel to our eyes.

Describe how light waves allow the boy to see with his periscope.

_____

_____

_____

_____

What if someone told you that the only **sounds** you experience take place inside your ears? In a way, they'd be right. If you pluck a stretched rubber band, it vibrates (moves back and forth). But it is not the rubber band vibrating that you hear. It is the air next to your ear that you hear. As the rubber band vibrates, it causes the air particles right next to it to vibrate. Those air particles cause the ones next to them to vibrate, and so on until the particles of air right next to your ear make your eardrum vibrate. Sound vibrations need matter to travel through; this matter is called a **medium**. Sound travels through many media, including water and metal.

A vacuum is a place with no matter in it at all. Outer space is a vacuum in most places. Why can't sound travel through a vacuum?

_____

_____

_____

Heat energy moves between things that are at different temperatures. For example, ice melts when placed on a kitchen table because the table and air are at a higher temperature—they're warmer—than the ice. When things that are at different temperatures touch each other, heat energy moves from the hotter thing to the colder thing. Imagine walking outside on a bitterly cold day. On days like this, you feel the cold hitting you like a ton of bricks. But really, cold is just the absence of heat. What you feel is actually the quick movement of your body heat out of you, into the cold air. Either way, it's not too pleasant!

In the case of the ice cube sitting on the kitchen table, in which direction did heat move?

_____

Heat is released when two objects rub against each other, which is why rubbing your hands together helps warm them up. You probably know that some materials release heat when they burn. Other materials don't have to be set on fire to release heat; they just need to be combined with certain other materials. For example, perhaps you have used pocket warmers, which are little bags that warm up when you squeeze them in your hands. The squeezing causes two chemicals to combine and release heat.

Solar energy is a special form of energy that combines the properties of light and heat. Light and heat from the Sun constantly bathe the Earth. This energy allowed all life on Earth to form. Humans are exploring ways to use solar energy as a consistent power source. Many satellites and other spacecraft use large "wings" made up of solar panels to collect solar energy and convert it to electricity.

One of the most fascinating forms of energy is **magnetism**. What makes a magnet stick to the metal door of the refrigerator? All forms of matter contain charges that have north and south poles. Opposite poles attract each other, and like poles repel each other. In normal, nonmagnetic material, all these charges are jumbled up, so they cancel each other out. That is why you and your friends don't stick to metal. In magnetic materials, all the charges are lined up, so all the north charges are pointing in the same direction. The combined force from all these charges gives a magnet the ability to attract or repel some metals. Metals such as iron and cobalt can be made into magnets.

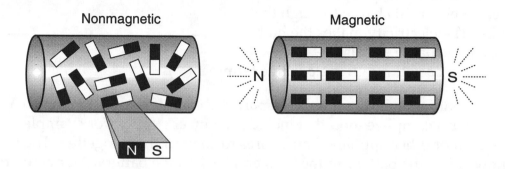

A close relative of magnetism is **electricity**, the movement of charges between objects. Like the poles of a magnet, opposite charges attract, and like charges repel. We all encounter electricity every day. When you receive a small shock of static electricity—perhaps after brushing your cat or walking across a carpet—you are experiencing the same thing that happens when lightning flashes in the sky. Both are movements of charged particles. Other forms of energy can be changed into electrical energy. For example, a battery changes chemical energy into electrical energy. The reverse is also possible; you can use electrical energy to "charge" a certain type of battery, restoring its chemical energy.

Water flowing through a dam can generate electricity. This is an example of mechanical energy changing into electricity. What other kinds of energy are transformed into electricity?

_____

_____

_____

_____

So how does the electricity travel from the electric company into our homes? If you imagine that the electric company is a simple battery and a house is a lightbulb, the whole idea becomes pretty simple. Batteries use electrical charges to make flashlights, games, and remote controls work. As the diagram to the right shows, you can use a battery to make a lightbulb glow. The negative terminal of the battery (−) pushes an electrical charge through the copper wire. The electricity makes the bulb light up, then the battery pulls the electrical charge back through the positive terminal (+).

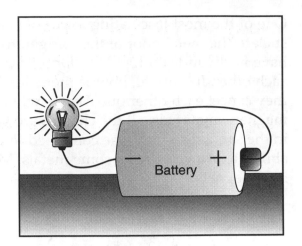

In order for a bulb to light up, it must be part of a complete loop, or circuit. A **closed circuit** is a complete loop that includes a power supply (for example, a battery), a bulb or other appliance, and wires to connect them together. The electric current flows from the battery to the bulb and back to the battery. An **open circuit** is a circuit that is broken or incomplete.

A bulb goes out when you turn off a light switch. What does this tell you about what the switch does?

_____

_____

_____

To make electricity travel, we need to use a **conductor**, which is any material that allows electrical charges to travel easily through it. Metal and water are two examples of conductors. This is why it is never a good idea to be near metal or water during a lightning storm. The difference between wild, dangerous lightning and the electricity coming into our homes is that we can control our electricity with **insulators**. Some materials, like rubber, glass, and wood, are good insulators. They do not easily let electrical charges travel through them.

Why do you think that people working on power lines wear heavy rubber gloves?

_____

_____

_____

Using What You Know

For this activity, you will need a ruler, a clock or stopwatch, light string or thread, a paper clip, and some metal washers or clay to hang on the string.

Step 1: Start with a piece of string that is about 30 cm long. Tie the paper clip onto one end of the string to make a bob. Pull the paper clip open slightly, to form a hook. Attach a washer or a piece of clay to the paper clip. Hold the other end of the string on the edge of a table so that the bob swings freely.

Step 2: Pull the bob back so that it is about 10 cm higher than its original position (check the height with your ruler). Then, release it. Using the table below, record how many seconds it takes for the bob to make 10 complete swings. (One complete swing is out and back.)

String Length (cm)	Description of Bob	Height Raised (cm)	Time Needed for 10 Swings (s)

Step 3: Pull the bob back so that it is about 15 cm higher than its original position (again, check the height with your ruler). Then, release it. Record how many seconds it takes for the bob to make 10 complete swings.

Step 4: Double the amount of clay or number of washers on the end of the string. Repeat Steps 2 and 3, and record the times in the table.

Step 5: Increase the length of the string by at least 15 cm, measuring with your ruler. Repeat Steps 2 and 3, and record the times in the table.

Think It Over

1. How much did the time for 10 swings change when you pulled the bob up higher?

   _____

2. How much did the time for 10 swings change when the bob weight was doubled?

   _____

3. How much did the time for 10 swings change when you increased the length of the string?

   _____

4. Which pendulum had the most potential energy?

   _____

Practice Questions

Directions: The diagram below shows one pendulum at three different positions during its swing. Use the diagram to answer Number 1.

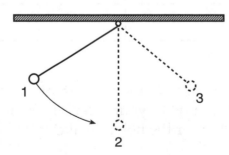

1. Which of the following statements is true about the energy of the pendulum bob when it is released from rest at position 1?
   A. The kinetic energy is greatest at the top of each swing.
   B. The kinetic energy is greatest at the bottom of each swing.
   C. The potential energy is greatest when the bob is moving the fastest.
   D. The potential and kinetic energy are equal at the bottom of each swing.

2. Which of the following is not a type of energy?

    A. solar

    B. electrical

    C. reflection

    D. chemical

3. What is the correct term for a material that allows heat or electricity to move through it easily?

    _____

    _____

4. Explain the difference between an open and closed electrical circuit.

    _____

    _____

    _____

    _____

    _____

People in Science

When she was only 14, Dorothy Crowfoot set up a laboratory in her attic so she could do chemistry experiments. One of her favorite pastimes was to grow crystals. Her love of crystals led to a lifelong mission: She wanted to learn about the patterns of all kinds of crystals. When she grew older, she married Thomas Hodgkin and became the mother of three children. All along, she kept studying crystals. One of the crystals she studied was penicillin. Because of her work, we now have different kinds of penicillin that can be used to kill deadly bacteria and save people's lives. In 1964, Dorothy Crowfoot Hodgkin received the Nobel Prize in Chemistry, one of the world's highest awards.

Dorothy Crowfoot Hodgkin
(England 1910–1994)

Review 13

Changes in Energy

You probably know that cars, trucks, and other vehicles are powered by gasoline. Similarly, coal and oil can be used to cool your home, run your refrigerator, and even power your video games. But wait—how does a clear, brownish liquid cause a truck that weighs thousands of pounds to cruise down a freeway? How do these ordinary-looking substances change to create the energy we use? And what will happen when supplies of gas, coal, and oil run out? This review will help you think about these questions.

What Do You Think?

Fossil fuels include crude oil, natural gas, and coal.

Explain how you think these fuels form underground.

_____

_____

_____

_____

_____

_____

What People Think

Energy is the ability to make things move or change. It is very difficult to think of any event happening in our daily lives that doesn't involve energy. As you learned in Review 12, energy affects matter in many ways. For example, we see bright light and feel heat when electricity goes through a lightbulb. Our skin feels the heat coming out of an oven. We hear sound when a saxophone player pushes air through her instrument. Energy makes things happen.

Key Words

electricity

energy

energy transformation

fossil fuel

nonrenewable energy

nuclear energy

renewable energy

turbine

Energy can have harmful effects, as well. Electricity and heat can shock and burn our skin. Loud sounds can damage our eardrums. The solar energy that brings life to the planet is also dangerous: Too much sunlight can burn our skin and cause disease.

Energy can change from one type to another. Each change is called an **energy transformation**. Mechanical energy changes to sound when you clap your hands. A doorbell changes an electrical current into sound. Solar panels change solar energy into electricity. Our bodies change chemical energy (food) into heat, mechanical, and other forms of energy.

List five other examples of energy transformations in your daily life.

_____

_____

_____

_____

_____

Many of the devices in our homes are powered by **electricity**. If you've ever experienced a power outage (such as the one in August 2003!), then you know just how important electricity is to the way we live. There are many types of energy, but electricity is especially important to our society because it can be easily transformed into many of the other types of energy. In our homes, we transform electricity into heat, light, and mechanical energy when we use electronic devices. Electricity is easier to store and transport than most other types of energy, which makes it especially useful. You can think of electricity as a form of currency, like dollars or pesos: It is easy to save it and change it into other things.

Name three different transformations that electricity goes through inside your home, and briefly explain how you use each transformation.

_____

_____

_____

_____

Life depends on a steady supply of energy. Organisms transform chemical energy into the heat and mechanical energy that they need to stay alive. In Reviews 16 and 17, you will explore how energy flows through a community of living things, called an *ecosystem*. This review focuses on nonliving sources of energy—or once-living sources, such as fossil fuels.

Knowing about energy transformations is quite important when discussing **renewable** and **nonrenewable energy** resources. Looking at their names, what do you think the difference is between a renewable and a nonrenewable source of energy?

_____

_____

_____

_____

As the name implies, **fossil fuels** such as crude oil, natural gas, and coal were formed from the remains of once-living organisms. The organisms that decayed to form fossil fuels got their energy either directly or indirectly from the Sun. Plants used sunlight for photosynthesis, and animals used the plants for food. You could say that fossil fuels are really sources of trapped sunshine. The processes that produced these fossil fuels are either no longer occurring, or they take so long that, for all practical purposes, these fuels are nonrenewable.

The United States uses more than 60% of its petroleum for transportation—mostly to power automobiles. Some people think that when our supplies of fossil fuels are exhausted, we can simply move from this energy resource to electricity. But more than 70% of our electricity is produced from coal, oil, and natural gas. These energy resources are used to turn water into steam that then turns a turbine. A **turbine** is a device that produces electricity when it is turned. Car engines, windmills, and many other electricity producers all contain turbines.

How can a radio, elevator, light, computer, or photocopier be thought of as running on fossil fuels?

_____

_____

_____

Several energy alternatives can be used to heat water to produce steam that will turn a turbine. For instance, the illustration to the right shows a geothermal power plant. In this type of power plant, the heat inside the Earth is used to produce the steam needed to turn the turbine.

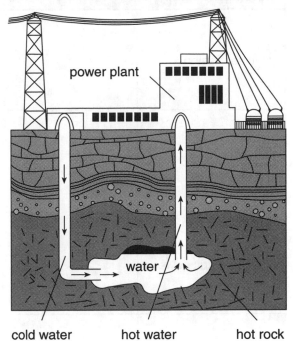

Geothermal Power Plant

power plant

water

cold water   hot water   hot rock

There are several other energy alternatives, and it is important to know how these resources can be managed. Solar energy is a unique and promising energy source because it is quite plentiful and produces little pollution. Some forms of solar energy can be converted to electricity without a turbine, whereas other forms turn water into steam that then turns a turbine. With **nuclear energy**, the nuclear fuel produces the heat necessary to create the steam that turns turbines. Other alternative energy sources, such as wind and running water (hydroelectric power), directly turn turbines.

What roles must science, technology, and society play in helping to solve our problem of vanishing energy sources?

_____

_____

_____

Using What You Know

Your teacher will assign you and a partner one of the alternative energy sources in the table on the following page. Use reference books and other sources of information to investigate advantages and disadvantages of your assigned alternative energy source.

After you have finished your section of the table, share the information with other groups. Complete the rest of the table for all the alternative energy sources. A blank box is provided if you wish to investigate another alternative energy source.

Alternative Energy	Advantages	Disadvantages
Nuclear fission		
Nuclear fusion		
Hydroelectric power		
Geothermal power		
Wind energy		
Solar energy		
Biomass fuel (e.g., wood, crop wastes)		

Think It Over

1. Is there any listed energy alternative that has no disadvantages? Explain how this observation applies to the need for energy resources and their availability.

_____

_____

_____

_____

_____

2. How is the Sun's energy responsible for fossil fuel, wind power, and hydroelectric energy?

_____

_____

_____

3. If alternative energy sources were to eventually replace fossil fuels, what would car manufacturers be forced to do?

_____

_____

_____

4. Imagine that a combination of alternative energy sources completely solved our energy needs. What reason would you still have to conserve energy?

_____

_____

_____

Practice Questions

1. Which one of these alternative energy sources can produce electricity without a turbine?

   A. wind

   B. solar

   C. water

   D. nuclear

2. What advantage does solar energy have over fossil fuels?

   A. Solar energy is more reliable and less expensive.

   B. Solar energy is less expensive and is transportable.

   C. Solar energy can be used anywhere and at any time.

   D. Solar energy is renewable and produces little pollution.

3. Suppose you eat a chocolate bar, run up a hill, and then roll down it. Which of the following describes the energy changes that took place?

   A. electrical → kinetic → potential → kinetic

   B. chemical → kinetic → potential → electrical

   C. chemical → kinetic → potential → kinetic

   D. solar → kinetic → potential → kinetic

4. Artemis is practicing her archery, and she shoots an arrow into the bull's-eye of the target. What statement best describes the movement of the energy?

   A. All the energy disappears when the arrow hits the target.

   B. The kinetic energy of the flying arrow is absorbed by the target.

   C. The arrow's potential energy causes the target to move when it hits.

   D. Kinetic energy from the archer produces potential energy in the arrow.

5. Describe the energy transformations that occur between a coal-burning power plant and the light you turn on at night.

   _____

   _____

   _____

   _____

Force and Motion

Do you ever think about whether the things that happen in cartoons could happen in real life? Some amazing things happen in cartoons, such as when Wile E. Coyote runs off a cliff and stays up in the air without falling—until he looks down. Things work differently in real life, of course. In the next few pages, you'll look at how objects really move. As you'll see, there is a regular pattern to the way that moving objects behave. That doesn't spoil the fun of cartoons, though!

What Do You Think?

There are lots of moving things around us. The following table lists some of them. Fill in the table by describing each object's motion and what makes that object move. An example is already filled in for you.

Moving Object	Describe the Motion	What Makes It Move?
A person on a swing	back and forth	gets a push or pumps with legs
A person sliding down a slide		
A person riding a bicycle		
A leaf falling from a tree		
A person riding a merry-go-round		
The hands on a clock		

Key Words

contact force	gravity	motion
force	lever	noncontact force
friction	machine	relative motion
fulcrum		

What People Think

Motion is the change in an object's position over time. You have probably heard someone use the term *miles per hour* when describing the speed of a car. If a car is traveling 20 miles per hour, this means that its position will change by 20 miles after 1 hour.

Rodney's pet snail has escaped! It is currently moving across a checkerboard. Use the following diagram to describe how the snail's position changes over time.

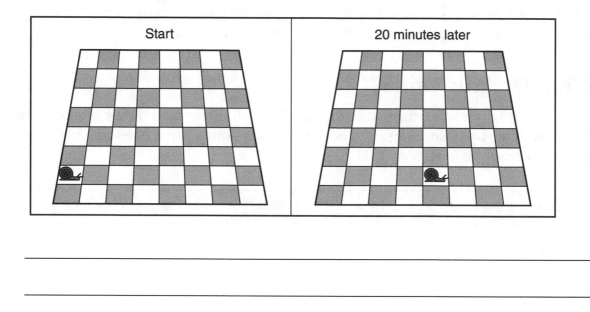

So, how do you know if something is moving or not? Scientists always describe the motion of something by comparing it to something else. This is called **relative motion**. On Earth, moving things are most often compared to the ground. For example, when you walk or run, you are moving compared to the ground, which stays in the same place. But motion can also be measured by making comparisons to things other than the ground. Think about walking in the aisle of a moving school bus. You are moving compared to the back or the front of the school bus, and the bus is moving compared to the ground. (Of course, you should never walk on a moving school bus.)

Suppose you got on a school bus and started walking to the back of the bus while the bus was beginning to move slowly forward. How would your motion look to someone sitting on the bus?

How would your motion look to someone standing on the ground outside the school bus?

_____

_____

_____

Think about riding a bicycle or skateboard on a level street. You have to start pedaling or pushing with your foot to start moving. You provide a **force**. It takes a force to change the motion of things. Before you push or pedal, you have no motion. If you do nothing, you continue to stand still. Once you give some force, your motion changes: You move.

Just as it takes a force to start something moving, it also takes a force to stop something or to change its motion. For example, when a moving object hits another object, the force of the collision changes the motion of both objects.

What happens to the ball and the bat when a baseball player swings and gets a hit?

_____

_____

_____

Many forces act at once on a moving object. For example, gravity pulls it toward the Earth, and friction works to slow it down. **Friction** is a force that acts between two objects or substances that are in contact with each other. Friction slows down movement, as the surfaces of the two objects catch on one another. No surface is perfectly smooth. You could hold a hand lens up to a block of ice or a skate blade and see that there are tiny bumps in each. So even while you are ice-skating, friction works to slow down your movement.

A force that must directly touch another object to affect it is a **contact force**. Friction and mechanical energy are examples of contact forces. Some forces do not need two objects to touch to make things change. These are called **noncontact forces**. Right now, a noncontact force is acting on you to keep you from floating off into space: **gravity**. When you are on a hill, you can just get on the bike and start moving, even if you don't pedal or push. This is because gravity makes you move. No one knows exactly what gravity is, but we do know that things attract, or pull, each other. We call this pull gravity. Noncontact forces such as gravity and magnetism work through gases, liquids, and solids. A magnet will attract a paper clip even through a piece of paper.

Max's father accidentally dropped some metal paper clips behind his desk. Max saw him tie a small rectangular object to a string, dangle it behind the desk, and pick up the paper clips. What noncontact force was used to pick up the paper clips?

_____

_____

When we describe the motion of objects, we must include how fast something is going as well as which direction it is going. For example, we compare the speed of objects by saying one moves slowly and another quickly. We can describe a moving object's direction by using words such as *up, down, left, right, north,* or *south.*

Look at the motions of the balls below. The longer the arrow is, the faster that ball is moving. How would you describe the motion of the balls? What direction is the fastest ball moving? What direction is the slowest ball moving?

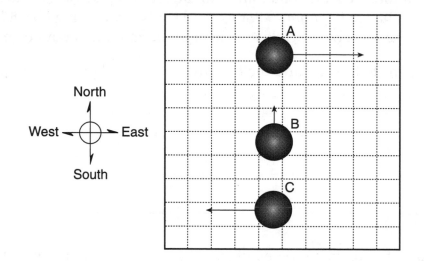

_____

_____

_____

_____

_____

A **machine** is anything that helps us do work with less force or with greater speed. For example, a shovel is a machine because it helps you move material like dirt or snow faster than you could do it with your hands. The bigger the shovel is, the more dirt or snow you can move at a time. Below you can see some simple machines.

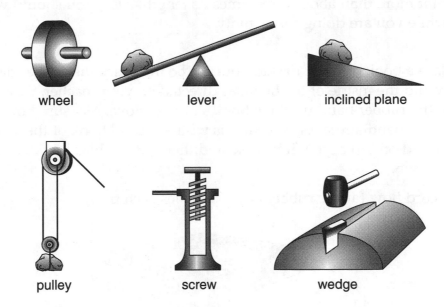

wheel   lever   inclined plane

pulley   screw   wedge

On the lines that follow, imagine what problem might have led to each invention listed, and then name one modern invention that is based on it.

Wheel: *moving heavy objects over long distances; the automobile*

Lever: _____

Inclined plane: _____

Pulley: _____

A canoe paddle, a wheelbarrow, and a board on a **fulcrum** (the point the board rests on, like what holds a seesaw up) are all simple machines that use **levers**. Wheels, axles, and ramps are also examples of simple machines. All machines need force in order to work. They need some kind of push or pull. Sometimes, an engine provides the force. Other times, nature or people provide the force.

Name as many simple machines as you can within a lawn mower.

_____

_____

What provides the force that makes a windmill go around?

_____

Using What You Know

A rubber band can be used to measure force. The farther you stretch a rubber band, the more force it takes to stretch it. To avoid snapping the rubber band, you should never stretch it more than about three times its length. Also, you should wear eye protection while you are doing this activity.

Step 1: Place a book on your desktop or on a board. Place the rubber band around the inside of the book, as directed by your teacher. Slowly pull on the rubber band until the book starts to move. Measure how far the rubber band stretches. Repeat this with a second book of the same size stacked on top of the first book, and then with a third book on top of the first two.

Record how far the rubber band stretches each time.

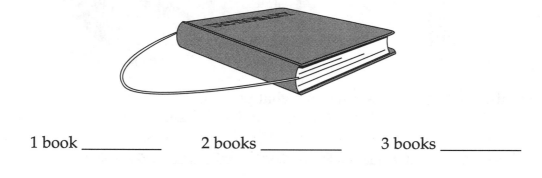

1 book _____   2 books _____   3 books _____

Step 2: Place a row of straws or wooden dowels between your book and the desktop. Pull the book with the rubber band. Measure how far the rubber band stretches. Repeat with two and three books.

1 book _____   2 books _____   3 books _____

Step 3: Lift one end of the desktop or board and place something under it, so it is at an angle. Use the same books and rubber band that you used in Step 1. Do not use the straws or dowels. Start the book at the bottom of the slide, and slowly pull the book up the slide with the rubber band. Measure how far the rubber band stretches. Repeat with two and three books.

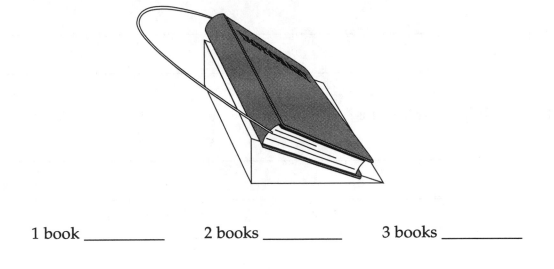

1 book _____   2 books _____   3 books _____

Think It Over

1. What was different about how far the rubber band stretched when you tried to pull one, two, and three books across the level surface?

   _____

   _____

   _____

   _____

2. How do you explain this?

   _____

   _____

   _____

   _____

3. What was different about pulling the books across the dowels or straws and pulling them across the desktop?

_____

_____

_____

_____

4. How do you explain this?

_____

_____

_____

_____

5. What was different about pulling the books up the slide rather than pulling them across the level surface?

_____

_____

_____

_____

6. How do you explain this?

_____

_____

_____

_____

Practice Questions

Directions: Use the following diagram to answer Number 1.

1. A raft is floating in a pool. What will happen to the raft if someone jumps onto it as shown in the diagram?

   A. It will remain at rest.

   B. It will turn in a circle.

   C. It will move toward the left in the diagram.

   D. It will move toward the right in the diagram.

Directions: Think about swimming in a flowing river. Use the drawings below to answer Number 2. The current in the river is flowing top to bottom in the diagrams.

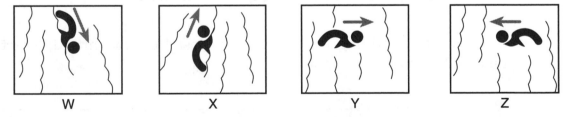

2. All four swimmers can swim at the same speed under equal conditions. Which swimmer will swim the fastest in the situation shown in the pictures?

   A. W

   B. X

   C. Y

   D. Z

Directions: Use the picture of a wheelbarrow shown here to answer Number 3.

3. Where should you place a load in a wheelbarrow to make it easiest to lift?
   A. position W
   B. position X
   C. position Y
   D. position Z

4. Which of the following is an example of a noncontact force?
   A. a boy pushing a door so that it opens
   B. a girl kicking a soccer ball so that it sails high into the air
   C. a magnet pulling on a bolt located a few inches away
   D. a hammer striking a nail and pushing it into some wood

5. Suppose you are slowly riding a bike toward the east. Describe three different ways you could change your motion.

UNIT 4

Life Science

Review 15

Basic Needs of Living Things

People need certain things in order to survive—things like food, water, clean air, and shelter. Animals, plants, and other **organisms** have the very same **basic needs**. They need to eat, drink, and breathe. They also need shelter from the weather, natural disasters (such as hurricanes and floods), and predators. All organisms have special features, called **characteristics**, that help them meet one or more of their basic needs. Nature usually doesn't "waste time" giving an organism a characteristic that doesn't help it survive in some way. In this review, you will look closely at the starting point of life science: the basic needs of living things.

Key Words

basic need	living	organism
cell	nonliving	shelter
characteristic	nutrient	thrive

What Do You Think?

Think about two different things: one that you would say is **living** and one that you would say is **nonliving**. Write each one on the correct line provided. On the lines marked *Characteristics*, list the characteristics each thing has that help you know whether it is living or nonliving.

Living thing: _____

Characteristics: _____

_____

Nonliving thing: _____

Characteristics: _____

_____

Compare your lists with other students' lists. Did they list any characteristics for their living or nonliving things that you did not? Are there any characteristics that you wrote down for one of the lists that someone else wrote down for the other list?

_____

_____

Is it a problem if a certain characteristic appears in both a "living thing" list and a "nonliving thing" list? Why do you think this?

_____

_____

What People Think

Probably the most important thing to know about living things is that they are made up of **cells**. Bacteria have just one cell. Larger life-forms, like trees or humans or whales, have trillions. Cells are the engines of living things. What does this mean? Well, think about a car engine. It turns gasoline into the energy needed to drive around, to keep the car warm, to charge the battery, and so on. Similarly, cells turn food into the energy that living things need to grow, to repair injuries, to respond to their surroundings, and so on. An engine that does not get enough fuel will stop working. A cell that does not get enough "fuel" (food, water, and so on) will die. Car engines and cells also produce waste products—substances that must be gotten rid of. For example, plants make a waste product called *oxygen*, and animals make a waste product called *carbon dioxide*.

If something is to be classified as living, it should have all of the following characteristics:

- It is made up of cells.
- It needs water and food in order to live.
- It grows.
- It reproduces itself.
- It responds to changes in the place where it lives.
- It gives off wastes.

Almost every living thing—from the tiniest one-celled organism to the largest animal—does all of these things to meet the basic needs of life. Living things can go without shelter, food, and water for a period of time, but to **thrive** (to grow and stay healthy), a living thing needs all these things. In Review 16, you'll learn about the life cycles of plants and animals, how they grow and reproduce. In Reviews 17 and 18, you'll look at how an organism's body parts (structures) help it fulfill its basic needs. In Reviews 19 and 20, you'll learn how different organisms respond to changes in their environments, the places where they live.

Think about the basic needs of food, water, and growth. How do you meet those needs? Do you meet them by yourself, or do others help you?

_____

_____

_____

_____

When you say, "I'm going home," what do you really mean? You probably mean that you are going to the house or apartment where you and your family eat, sleep, and keep all the things you own. Scientifically, you mean that you are going to the place that you use as **shelter**.

What are some things that your home shelters you from?

_____

_____

Different animals have different kinds of shelters. Animals use their shelters for many different things. Shelters protect animals from rain, wind, heat, and cold. Shelters also protect animals from their enemies.

Like people, some animals build their own shelters. One animal that does this is the beaver. Beavers use the wood from trees they have cut down, along with rocks and mud, to build their shelters. These shelters, called *lodges*, are built in water. The inside area where the beavers live is above the surface level of the water. Small holes between the logs and branches in the ceiling let in fresh air. The entrances to the inside area are all below the surface of the water. This means that beavers have to swim to get home.

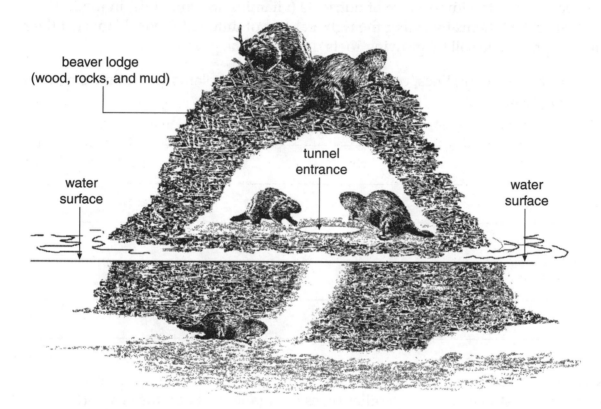

Why is the inside room of a beaver lodge above the surface of the water?

_____

_____

How do the underwater entrances protect the beavers from some of their enemies?

_____

_____

Not all animals build their own shelters. Bats and some bears, for example, use caves as shelters. Many snakes live in holes that other animals have left. Some kinds of fish use coral reefs or underwater plants as shelters. Shelters do more than keep animals comfortable and safe. They also give the animals a good place to raise offspring.

Plants have the same basic needs as animals, but they satisfy these needs in different ways. Animals must consume other living things (plants, animals, fungi, and so on) for their food, but plants use sunlight to produce their own food. The energy in sunlight causes special cells in a plant to create sugars, which the plant uses for food. Plants "breathe," too: Land plants need clean air, and aquatic (underwater) plants need clean water. Just like animals, plants need **nutrients** to grow. In Review 16, you will learn about the importance of nutrients (vitamins and minerals) in food. Animals get nutrients by eating the right balance of different foods. Plants get their nutrients from the soil by growing roots down into the ground.

On the following lines, compare and contrast how plants and animals meet their basic needs.

_____

_____

_____

_____

_____

_____

No organism can survive without other living things. To live and thrive, an organism must live near many other types of organisms. Sometimes a particular plant or animal depends directly on other plants or animals. A koala, for example, is completely dependent on the eucalyptus (YOO cuh LIP tuss) tree for its food; the eucalyptus leaves make up the majority of the koala's diet. These leaves are poisonous to most animals, but the koala's stomach is adapted to digest these leaves. Because no other animals eat the eucalyptus leaves, the koala has a plentiful supply of food. However, if the eucalyptus trees in an area are cut down, then the koalas will either die or move to another area with these trees.

Humans depend on many other organisms to thrive. Plants and certain types of bacteria process sunlight and give off oxygen as a result. Billions of years ago, there was no oxygen in the Earth's atmosphere, so animals could not live. Gradually, bacteria gave off enough oxygen to allow animals to form. Today, we still rely on plants and bacteria to give off a steady supply of oxygen. In Review 20, you'll take a closer look at how living things depend on each other.

Using What You Know

Think about the living organisms shown near and in the pond.

Step 1: Put all the living things into two categories: plants and animals.

Plants: _____

_____

Animals: _____

_____

Step 2: Using outside resources such as the library or the Internet, find out how each pond organism in the following table finds its food, water, and protection. Complete the table.

Organism	Food Source	Water Source	Protection
Trees			
Cattails			
Frog			
Raccoon			

Think It Over

1. What do you notice about the food source for the plants?

   _____

   _____

2. Why do all these organisms live near or in the pond?

   _____

   _____

3. Where, in or around a pond, would you most likely find frog eggs? Where would you most likely find tadpoles? Where can adult frogs go that eggs or tadpoles cannot?

Eggs are found: _____

Tadpoles are found: _____

Frogs can go: _____

Practice Questions

1. How does a cobra's poisonous venom help it to meet a basic need?
   A. The venom is used to create the cells that make up the cobra's body.
   B. The cobra uses the venom to kill its prey, allowing the snake to eat.
   C. The venom helps the cobra dissolve wastes that it produces in its body.
   D. Cobras with lots of venom attract more mates, allowing them to reproduce.

2. All living things need food to continue living. Why, then, must you give food to a pet hamster, but you don't need to give food to a plant?
   A. Plants are not living things.
   B. Plants digest food from the air.
   C. Plants can live longer without food.
   D. Plants make their own food using the energy from sunlight.

3. A scientist in Antarctica looked underneath a frozen rock and discovered a greenish substance called a *lichen*. How did she decide to classify it, and why?
   A. living, because it was green
   B. living, because she could observe cell growth
   C. nonliving, because it could not move by itself
   D. nonliving, because it's too cold for anything to live in Antarctica

4. Why do many wild animals live near a river, lake, or stream?

   _____

   _____

   _____

Plant and Animal Life Cycles

All living organisms go through a life cycle. They live, grow, reproduce, and die. This pattern of changes allows every species to continue from one generation to the next. It also keeps each species from having too many members and overcrowding the Earth. In this review, you will learn about the life cycles of plants and animals.

What Do You Think?

List members of your family in the chart, starting with yourself. Describe the hair color, hair type (straight, wavy, curly, and so on), and eye color for each person.

Family Members' Hair and Eye Chart

Family Member	Hair Color	Hair Type	Eye Color
Me			

Key Words

drug	larva	pollen
drug abuse	life cycle	pupa
extinct	metamorphosis	reproduce
food guide pyramid	nutrition	species
hygiene	offspring	vitamin

Which, if any, of these characteristics change naturally in a person?

_____

_____

_____

_____

You know that human beings change as they grow and age. Other animals change in even bigger ways. Sometimes these changes can be so big that it seems like the animal is turning into a different kind of living thing. When an organism goes through a change this big, it is called a **metamorphosis**.

What are some examples of organisms that go through a metamorphosis?

_____

_____

What People Think

A **species** is a group of living things that can reproduce itself over generations. Each population of species has to survive long enough to **reproduce** itself. Otherwise, that species disappears (becomes extinct). For example, not every raccoon has to reproduce, but the whole population of raccoons has to produce enough healthy **offspring**, or babies, to replace the raccoons that die from old age or other causes. Likewise, not every pine tree in a forest needs to produce young trees, but some trees in the forest need to produce young trees to maintain the forest.

All living things go through a **life cycle**. Generally, all living things begin life, they grow, they reproduce, and they die. Living things must have a steady source of food energy to survive. Energy from food helps all living things repair their bodies and grow. Of course, the life cycle of a plant is a lot different than the life cycle of an animal. The main difference between plants and animals is that plants can make their own food, but animals cannot. This leads to very different life cycles.

Consider the life cycle of a flowering plant, which begins as a seed. There are many different kinds of seeds. For example, the seed could be a bit of dandelion fluff, a speck inside a pinecone, or a peach pit. Once the seed is in a good spot—with warm temperatures, enough water, and the right kind of soil—it will sprout. After a period of growth, the young plant will begin to flower. These flowers exchange **pollen** with other flowers, which allows them to develop seeds. The seeds scatter in a variety of ways to begin new plants. Some plants only live for a year, but they produce enough seeds during that time to keep the species alive. Other plants live a lot longer. In fact, the oldest living thing on Earth is a bristlecone pine tree living in Utah named Methuselah. Methuselah is almost 5,000 years old!

In the following box, sketch and label the four main stages in a plant's life cycle. You may draw any plant you choose.

Animals have widely varying life cycles. Animals either hatch from an egg or are born. Many animals care for their young until they are large enough to defend themselves. Many insects and amphibians go through metamorphoses, so the young look and act very differently than the adults. Once an animal grows into adulthood, it will likely reproduce and bear offspring. Like plants, there is a great variety of life spans in animals. Many insects, for example, only live one day, whereas the giant tortoise can live for more than 150 years.

To continue living in its environment, each species has adapted special ways to find food, defend itself, build a home, and create the next generation. Species are not always successful at making the next generation, however. When the organisms in a population die off faster than they reproduce, that species eventually becomes **extinct**. Normal changes in a species' surroundings—such as seasonal temperature changes, flooding, or a shortened food supply—usually won't cause a species to become extinct. Extinction most often occurs because of habitat destruction, which results in the disappearance of the species' source of food and shelter.

For each living organism listed below, describe how the young are protected by the parent.

Baby bird: _____

Human child: _____

Sea turtle: _____

Salmon: _____

Protecting the young helps each species to survive in its environment. Not all organisms look after their offspring, however. Plants cannot take care of young plants, and many animals leave their young as soon as they are born (or the eggs are laid). Such organisms generally produce many offspring. They do this because not all of the offspring that are produced will survive. If many are produced, there is a better chance that some will grow to adulthood.

About how many acorns (seeds) do you think an oak tree produces each year?

_____

About how many new oak trees sprout around the oak tree each year?

_____

Most species of fish, insects, and plants produce numerous offspring, but most of those offspring die. This may sound sad, but in many ways it is a good thing. Think about this: If every egg produced by every fly were somehow to survive to become an adult, within a couple of years, the entire Earth would be covered with a layer of flies about 3 feet deep! That's a pretty gross example, but it points out why it is important that not all offspring survive.

You are currently in the growth phase of your life cycle. This is an extremely important time for you. There are many practices that you should follow so that you can reach the adult stage as healthy and strong as possible.

Eating healthy food provides your body with the right materials to grow, repair itself, and fight off disease. Not just any food will do, however. **Nutrition**, the study of healthy eating, took an important step forward in the 1910s when vitamins were discovered. Before then, it was thought that food only provided energy. The discovery of **vitamins** showed that there are certain chemicals that are necessary for growth and a healthy body. Soon, food-makers began adding vitamins to their foods to increase their nutritional value.

Eating right involves both what we eat and how much we eat. The **food guide pyramid** below shows the familiar food groups.

U.S. Dept. of Agriculture Guide to Daily Food Choices

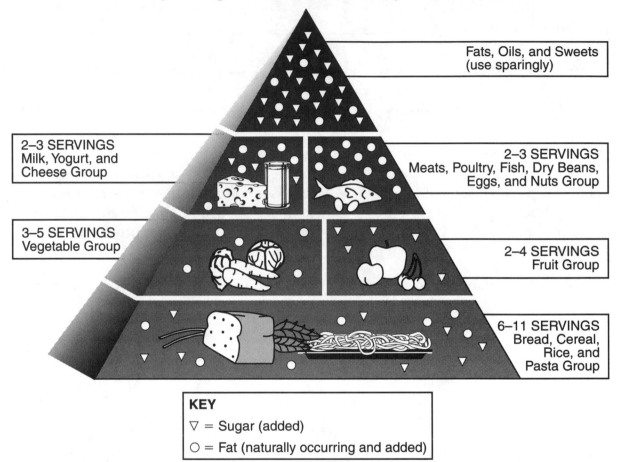

On the following lines, use the food guide pyramid to design a healthy evening meal that you would enjoy.

_____

_____

_____

Another important practice is exercise. If your body doesn't get regular exercise, it won't be as good at keeping itself healthy. Walking, playing sports, dancing—these are all great ways to stay healthy and strong. Sleep is also extremely important. Young people should get between 8 and 10 hours of sleep each night. Sleep helps keep the mind clear and the body healthy. It is also important to practice good **hygiene**, which is the way we clean our bodies and clothing. Washing your hands after using the bathroom and before every meal will help prevent disease. Taking a shower or bath every couple of days helps prevent skin infections.

Avoiding harmful materials is also important. Any nonfood chemical substance that changes the way the body functions is a **drug**. Not all drugs are harmful by themselves, but most drugs are harmful if taken in large quantities.

Using this definition, list all the substances around your home that would be considered drugs.

_____

_____

_____

List other substances that you know that might also be considered as drugs.

_____

_____

_____

_____

In many parts of the world, tobacco and alcohol are commonly used. People often do not think of these substances as drugs because they are widely available and are legal for adults. But alcohol and tobacco affect how the body works and are therefore drugs. Both of these substances damage the human body, and the effects are much worse on young bodies.

Drugs are often grouped as prescription drugs, over-the-counter drugs, or illegal drugs. Prescription drugs are bought at pharmacies and require a doctor's permission. Over-the-counter drugs can be bought at stores without a prescription. Illegal drugs include marijuana, cocaine, and heroin. When people think of **drug abuse**, they often think of illegal drugs. But *all* drugs can be misused and abused. To grow into a healthy adult, you should avoid illegal drugs and follow your doctor's instructions when taking prescription drugs.

Using What You Know

Your teacher will give you some mealworms in meal and a hand lens.

Step 1: Look carefully through the meal for anything that looks alive or like it might be related to the living things that you find. Draw what you find in the box below.

Step 2: Keep track of how many of each living thing you find in the meal. Name or describe them on the following lines.

_____

_____

_____

_____

Think It Over

1. What does the offspring of the mealworm species look like?

   _____

   _____

2. How is the baby produced in this species?

   _____

   _____

3. In the picture below, draw arrows that show the life cycle you think this mealworm species follows.

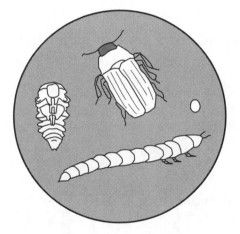

An insect goes through four stages in metamorphosis. In order from youngest to oldest, they are egg, **larva**, **pupa**, and adult. Go back to the picture of the mealworm's life cycle and write the name of the correct stage next to each illustration.

4. How is the life cycle of the mealworm similar to and different from the life cycle of a chicken? How is it similar to and different from the life cycle of a dog?

   Chicken: _____

   _____

   Dog: _____

   _____

Practice Questions

1. Look at the life cycle of a butterfly. During which part of the cycle does the insect lay its eggs?

       larva   pupa   adult   egg

   A. larva

   B. pupa

   C. adult

   D. egg

2. Which of the following creatures goes through a metamorphosis during its lifetime?

   A. human

   B. tadpole

   C. shark

   D. ostrich

3. What is the best way to avoid drug abuse?

   A. Never use any drug.

   B. Use only prescription drugs.

   C. Use only legal drugs as instructed.

   D. Use only over-the-counter drugs.

4. Every little white puff from a dried dandelion flower is a seed for another dandelion. Why are there so many dandelion seeds on each plant?

_____

_____

_____

_____

5. Using the space and lines below, compare the life cycle of a typical plant with the life cycle of a typical animal. You may use drawings, words, or both in your comparison.

_____

_____

_____

People in Science

Jane Goodall knew as a child in Great Britain that her life's work would be with animals. She loved to read animal books and study animals in nature. At age 23, she went to Africa to work with Dr. Louis Leakey. Dr. Leakey was a famous anthropologist (a person who studies the physical and cultural backgrounds of humans), and Goodall assisted Dr. Leakey in his search for fossils of early humans. Later, Dr. Leakey suggested that Goodall  work with live chimpanzees. Dr. Goodall found her career with that assignment. Her study of chimpanzees who live near Lake Tanganyika in what is now Tanzania is the longest continuous study of animals in their natural surroundings. Goodall discovered that chimps are complex, intelligent creatures with rich emotional lives. They have unique personalities. They also use tools and hunt in ways similar to humans. Today, Goodall travels the world, speaking about the importance of all life on this planet. She has helped raise human understanding of other animal life-forms.

Jane Goodall
(Great Britain 1934–)

Review 17

Structure and Function in Living Things

Can you imagine a seal trying to pick fruit with its flippers? How about a gorilla swimming deep under water, trying to catch a squid for dinner? Those animals would have a hard time getting enough to eat. Of course, nature doesn't work that way. Over thousands of years, seals have developed structures that make them experts at diving deep and catching fish. Likewise, gorillas survive really well in rain forests. Both animals are well suited to their own environments. Animals and plants have certain structures that help them fulfill their basic needs. In this review, you will learn about some plant and animal structures.

What Do You Think?

Plants are similar to animals in many ways. One important similarity is that both plants and animals have structures that help them survive and reproduce. Almost every feature you can see on a plant has a job that helps that plant. Look at this photograph of a palmetto, a type of palm tree.

What do you think are some structures that help the palmetto survive?

_____

_____

Key Words

camouflage	photosynthesis	seed
flower	pollen	stem
fruit	predator	vertebrate
leaf	root	

What People Think

Plants have developed many ways of getting their **seeds** out in the world. One way is to grow bright, nutritious **fruit**. Seeds grow within the fruit. Animals eat the fruit and spread its seeds around. In this way, plants have developed a kind of reward to animals for spreading their seeds. Other plants, such as maple trees and dandelions, have seeds that can float along with the wind. This feature allows the seeds to spread over a large area. All seed structures are designed to get seeds out into the world and grow a new plant of the same type.

Many types of plants have **flowers**. Like fruits, flowers often have colors or smells that attract certain types of animals, such as bees and hummingbirds. Plants attract these animals to their flowers to help them develop seeds through a kind of trade-off. For example, hummingbirds eat the nectar found in certain flowers. This provides the hummingbird with a high-energy food. In exchange, the flower coats the face and neck of the bird with its **pollen**, a powdery substance that causes seeds to form. Pollen must leave its original flower and travel to a different flower of the same species in order to start a seed. Sometimes the wind carries the pollen, and sometimes an animal provides the service.

Why are bees attracted to flowers?

_____

_____

_____

_____

_____

Plants perform one of the most amazing jobs in the world: They make their own food from sunlight, water, and carbon dioxide, a common gas found in the air. The **leaf** of a plant is where most of this action takes place. When sunlight hits a leaf, and there is enough water and carbon dioxide around, the leaf will make a type of sugar that can be used for energy. This process is called **photosynthesis**. (*Photo-* means *light*, and *-synthesis* means *making*.) Most life-forms on Earth get their energy from this amazing work performed by leaves.

It's easy to see how a plant can get all the sunlight and air it needs. But how does it get water? A plant's **roots** grow downward into the ground. If you dig a small hole in the ground and feel the soil, there is usually a little moisture there. The skin of a root is very good at absorbing water. Roots can even sense where water might be, and they will grow in that direction. The roots channel water up through the stem into the leaves, where it can be used to make food.

Stems do more than just connect the roots with the leaves. They bring water up to the leaves, and they move food to the roots, other branches, and leaves. Stems are also the growth centers for plants. Have you ever looked at the trunk of a tree that has been cut down? Each year, a tree grows from the inside of its trunk (its stem), and each new growth forms a ring inside of the trunk. Plants other than trees also grow from their stems.

Plant stems also provide protection. Name two different ways a stem can protect a plant.

_____

_____

_____

_____

Just like plants, animals have most of their structures for a good reason: to help the animal fulfill its basic needs. Think about your own body for a minute. There are very few "useless" structures. Humans have evolved thumbs, which helped our ancestors get food and make tools. Our large brains have allowed us to adapt to changing conditions in our environment. People have adapted to live in almost every type of region on Earth, from frozen Antarctica to the hottest deserts of Africa. We've even managed to get year-round residents living in outer space on the *International Space Station*.

Besides the brain and the thumb, describe another structure of humans and how it helps us meet a basic need.

_____

_____

_____

Identify how each of the following features helps the plant or animal during its life.

A rhinoceros's horn: _____

A snail's shell: _____

A cardinal's song: _____

Of course, there are a lot of differences between animal and plant structures. For one, many types of animals can move around. Wings, legs, and fins help some animals look for food and escape danger. Some animals are adapted to move long distances every year. You'll learn more about these movements in Review 19.

Unlike plants, animals must eat living things or materials produced by living things. To help them do this, animals have a wide variety of mouthparts. Fish, reptiles, mammals, birds, and amphibians have jaws that open and close. Birds do not have teeth, but their beaks come in many shapes and sizes, allowing different types of birds to eat many different things. Reptiles have sharp teeth that allow them to kill and eat other animals. Mammals have many different kinds of teeth. Horses and other plant-eaters have wide, flat teeth for crushing up plant leaves. Lions have sharp teeth for tearing up meat.

Like plants, animals sense their surroundings and respond to them. The structures that animals have to do this are very different from those of plants. An animal might use its eyes, nose, ears, tongue, or skin to sense its surroundings. Insects have antennae, or "feelers," that they use to sense their surroundings. Bats make sound waves that bounce off objects and return to the bat, giving it a "sound picture" of its world.

> For each animal, draw a line connecting it with the sense that it mainly uses to collect information.

Eagle	eyes
Dog	ears
Bat	tongue
Snake	nose

Many types of animals, including humans, use sounds to communicate. Dolphins use high-pitched squeals to organize each other during hunts. Birds have many different calls, each with its own meaning. Smell is very important in the animal world, too. Dogs, gorillas, and many other animals produce scents to mark their territory and to communicate with each other. Skunks actually use their scent as a defense.

Another way animals communicate is through the color of their skin. For example, certain frogs are brightly colored and poisonous. This acts as a kind of warning, telling **predators** (animals that eat other animals) that the frog is poisonous. Soon, the predator learns not to eat that type of frog. Other animals, especially fish and birds, use color as a way to attract mates.

Many animals are adapted to protect themselves from enemies by blending in with their environment. This is called **camouflage**. A dark moth, for example, is difficult to spot when it is resting on the brown bark of a tree. The photograph to the right shows a zebra. Even though the zebra appears very bright to our eyes, its black and white stripes are the perfect camouflage for the sunny grasslands where it lives.

A type of bird in the Arctic changes color with the seasons. It is brown in the summer and white in the winter. How does this help keep the bird safe?

_____

_____

_____

This review has introduced you to structures: what they are and how they help plants and animals survive. Scientists classify plants and animals by their various structures. The following table lists the main groups of **vertebrates**, the animals that have backbones. Use your own knowledge or outside sources (such as a textbook or dictionary) to provide the type of body covering for each group, as well as a body structure that is special for each group.

Vertebrate	Body Covering	Example of Body Structure
Bird		
Reptile		
Amphibian		
Mammal		
Fish		

Using What You Know

During this activity, you will study the structures of different plants.

Step 1: Look closely at the three plants that your teacher points out. Every kind of plant on Earth has structures that help it live in its environment.

In the space below, draw the plants you have observed.

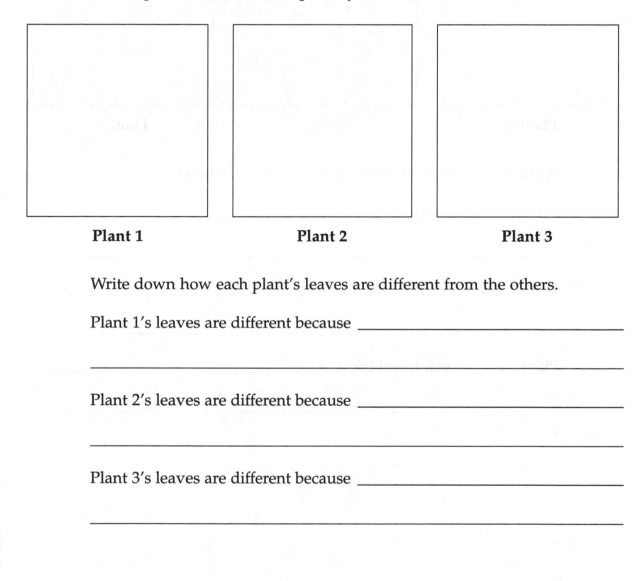

Plant 1   **Plant 2**   **Plant 3**

Write down how each plant's leaves are different from the others.

Plant 1's leaves are different because _____

_____

Plant 2's leaves are different because _____

_____

Plant 3's leaves are different because _____

_____

Step 2: Look closely at the stem of each plant. In the spaces below, draw a part of the stem of each plant.

Plant 1	**Plant 2**	**Plant 3**

Write down how each stem is different from the others.

Plant 1's stem is different because _____

_____

Plant 2's stem is different because _____

_____

Plant 3's stem is different because _____

_____

Think It Over

Directions: Use the illustrations below to answer Numbers 1 through 4.

Holly Tree

Oak Tree

Beech Tree

Catalpa Tree

Tulip Tree

Pine Tree

1. What is one special thing about each of these leaves?

Holly: _____

Oak: _____

Beech: _____

Catalpa: _____

Tulip: _____

Pine: _____

2. How would hard, sharp points on leaves help a plant survive?

_____

_____

_____

3. What function might the wide, flat shape of the catalpa leaf have to help the plant survive?

_____

_____

4. Select your favorite leaf drawing (catalpa, pine, holly, tulip, oak, or beech). What special adaptation does the leaf have to help the plant survive?

_____

_____

_____

Practice Questions

Directions: Use the drawing to the right to answer Numbers 1 through 3.

1. Which part of the plant brings in water and minerals?
   A. W
   B. X
   C. Y
   D. Z

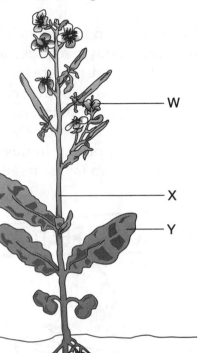

2. Which part of the plant contains reproductive structures?
   A. W
   B. X
   C. Y
   D. Z

3. Most of the photosynthesis occurs in which part of the plant?
   A. W
   B. X
   C. Y
   D. Z

4. A pheasant is a bird that lives in the woods and sometimes in farmers' fields. The female pheasant is brown and tan in color. What is the correct term for this type of coloring?
   A. response
   B. predator
   C. camouflage
   D. hibernation

5. Ducks' feet have webbing between the toes. How does this adaptation help ducks to survive?
   A. It helps them paddle across water.
   B. It helps them sit on branches in trees.
   C. It helps them catch food with their feet.
   D. It helps them attract a mate and have offspring.

Review 18

Inherited and Learned Characteristics

As you learned in Review 17, all of the millions of different kinds of living things in the world today have special **characteristics** that help them to survive. Some of these characteristics are inherited, which means they are passed from parent to child before birth. Some characteristics are learned, which means they result from contact with the environment. Humans have special characteristics, too. Some of these characteristics are the thumbs on our hands and the ability to learn language and to walk upright. In this review, you will look at how these characteristics develop over many generations, as living things interact with their environments.

Key Words

behavior	inherit	migration
characteristic	instinct	trait
environment	learned behavior	variation

What Do You Think?

Think about the bears you have seen in books, on television, or maybe at the zoo. Different kinds of bears live in different places. Each kind of bear has special characteristics that help it to survive wherever it lives.

Name the different bears that you have seen. What is special about them? Where do the bears that you have seen live?

_____

_____

_____

Could any of the bears survive if they switched where they lived with a different kind of bear? Why or why not?

_____

_____

_____

What People Think

You might think that any animal or plant can live in any place, but this is not true. The place where an organism lives is its **environment**. All of the living and nonliving things in an organism's environment affect it. As you learned in Review 17, organisms can respond to changes in their environments by slowly developing characteristics that help them survive. This takes many generations. These characteristics can be **inherited** by offspring from their parents. Inherited characteristics are called **traits**.

Can you name three different traits that a fish has? Think about where it lives, how it moves, and what it eats.

_____

_____

_____

Sometimes, an organism's characteristics change during its lifetime. In this case, the organism might be changing in a way that is not inherited from its parents. For example, people who work outside in the sunlight all their lives develop darker skin to prevent sunburns. You inherit intelligence from your parents, but the languages that you learn to speak are not inherited characteristics. In the plant world, a fern might inherit some characteristics from its parent, such as being delicate and sensitive to light. However, if the young fern is exposed to too much sunlight, it takes on a new characteristic: browned and wilted leaves.

What is one characteristic you possess that you did not inherit from your parents?

_____

_____

The way an animal reacts to changes is called a **behavior**. Behavior can develop over a shorter time than structural changes, which require many generations to take hold. Certain behaviors called **instincts** are automatic, and they happen without the animal thinking about them. Each year in the northern hemisphere, birds such as ducks and geese fly south for the winter. Then, when spring comes and the weather gets warm up north, they fly back home. This kind of journey is called a **migration**. You'll learn more about migrations in Review 19. Many different animals go on seasonal migrations for better feeding opportunities. These animals know when to migrate because their instincts tell them. Scientists don't have a full understanding of how instincts work.

Describe some instincts that people have that keep them safe.

_____

_____

Other, more complex behaviors are controlled by an animal's brain and nervous system. These are called **learned behaviors** because they must be taught. Now, it's hard to picture a group of hedgehogs sitting in a classroom, taking notes. But most animals with complex brains are capable of learning survival lessons during their lifetimes. A lizard may find that a certain bright-red insect is quite nasty to eat, so the lizard learns to avoid that insect. Some animals—such as deer, lions, and humans—learn from their parents.

Imagine that you just got a new puppy. What are some learned behaviors that you hope your puppy will gain?

_____

_____

_____

Traits and instinctive behaviors are inherited. Offspring frequently look like their parents, and they also have the same instincts. Each parent passes on some of its traits to the offspring, so that the offspring have some traits that match one or both parents. Some human examples of inherited traits, which you'll explore in the following activity, are eye color, hair color, attached earlobes, and the ability to roll one's tongue. Sometimes the offspring look different from their parents or from the other young. They may even act differently. Being different, or having **variation**, gives the whole species a better chance to survive. The more variations a species has, the better it can adapt to changes in the environment. Humans display variation all the time. For example, you may grow up to be taller than your parents, or you might develop an allergy that they do not have.

Think of a kind of bird that has very bright feathers that its enemies can easily see. Why are the offspring of this bird usually born with dull-colored feathers?

_____

_____

_____

_____

_____

Using What You Know

Some physical characteristics, such as hair color, are traits passed from parents to their offspring. Other traits are inherited, too. In this activity, you will explore some of the physical traits that humans inherit from their parents.

Step 1: Work with one or two partners to study five traits of the people in your classroom. The five traits you should study are shown in the illustrations below. Collect data about each trait, and record your data in the tables that follow on page 165. Put a tally mark in the correct box for each piece of information that you gather. Keep separate records for girls and for boys.

Trait #1   Trait #2   Trait #3   Trait #4   Trait #5

Trait 1, earlobes:
Check everyone's earlobes to see whether they are attached or unattached.

Trait 2, dimples:
Check everyone for little indentations in the chin or cheeks.

Trait 3, arm crossing:
Have everyone fold their arms across their chests and note which arm is on top.

Trait 4, tongue rolling:
See whether people can curl the edges of their tongues upward.

Trait 5, widow's peak:
Check for a downward point in the middle of the hairline on the forehead. If the hairline goes straight across the top of the forehead, it is not a widow's peak.

Traits of Girls

Trait 1: Earlobes	Trait 2: Dimples	Trait 3: Arm Crossing	Trait 4: Tongue Rolling	Trait 5: Widow's Peak
attached:	dimples:	right over left:	can roll:	widow's peak:
unattached:	no dimples:	left over right:	cannot roll:	no widow's peak:

Traits of Boys

Trait 1: Earlobes	Trait 2: Dimples	Trait 3: Arm Crossing	Trait 4: Tongue Rolling	Trait 5: Widow's Peak
attached:	dimples:	right over left:	can roll:	widow's peak:
unattached:	no dimples:	left over right:	cannot roll:	no widow's peak:

Step 2: If your teacher assigned you only a certain trait or two to research, exchange data with other groups to complete your tables.

Think It Over

1. Which trait or traits are the same for most students in your classroom?

   _____

   Do your data show any differences between boys and girls for these traits? If so, which traits?

   _____

   _____

2. What is one characteristic of your physical appearance that is not a trait that can be inherited from your parents?

   _____

3. How might something like the size or position of an animal's ears help or hurt its chances for survival?

   _____

   _____

   _____

4. What kind of special trait would help an animal survive in a place that has a lot of soft, marshy ground?

   _____

   _____

   _____

Practice Questions

1. Which of the following behaviors is an instinct?
   A. a cat using a litter box
   B. a chimpanzee using sign language
   C. a dog begging for food at the dinner table
   D. a male grasshopper rubbing its legs together to attract a female

2. Which of the following behaviors is not an instinct?
   A. geese migrating south for winter
   B. eagles building nests on high cliffs and trees
   C. a grizzly bear cub fishing after watching its mother
   D. baby sea turtles running to the sea after hatching

3. Which of the following variations would probably help a baby bird to survive in the woods of the northern United States?
   A. having white feathers
   B. having very brightly colored feathers
   C. having more feathers than its brothers and sisters
   D. having feathers that blend in with the area where it lives

4. Frogs live in many parts of the world. Some have webbed feet; others have separated toes. What difference do you think this makes in the way these frogs live?

   _____

   _____

   _____

5. An adult chimpanzee shows a young chimpanzee over and over how to dig for bugs with a stick. Is this an example of instinct or of learned behavior? Explain your answer.

   _____

   _____

   _____

   _____

Review 19

Responding to Change

The Serengeti National Park in Tanzania, Africa, is home to thousands of different plants and animals. Strangely, though, it's not a very easy place to live for all these organisms. In fact, the seasons change dramatically every year, going from severe drought to heavy rains and flooding. The organisms that live there have developed many curious ways of dealing with these changes. Some animals migrate long distances during the dry periods to get to water, and some animals bury themselves underground and try to sleep through it! The plants, of course, don't have the option of moving to a different place: They're stuck. But as you'll see, plants have also developed many ways of dealing with all kinds of change.

What Do You Think?

For two mornings in a row, Rahim noticed a rabbit that was looking for food in his mother's garden. On the second day, his mother put up a fence. The next morning, Rahim saw that the rabbit had moved over to the neighbor's garden. Then he began to wonder what his mother's flowers did when they needed to find new sources of food and water.

This picture shows a young, healthy flowering plant in the springtime. Is it moving? Draw arrows on the picture to show how it is moving, and describe the movements on the lines below.

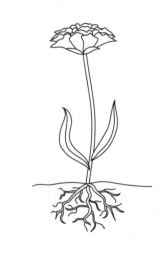

Key Words

adapt

behavior

competition

external stimulus

extinct

habitat

hibernation

instinct

internal stimulus

migration

resource

stimulus

_____

_____

_____

What do you think causes the plant to move in this way?

_____

_____

_____

What People Think

All organisms respond to **stimuli** (the plural form of *stimulus*). Stimuli are changes that cause a change in **behavior**. **External stimuli** come from the environment, and **internal stimuli** come from within an organism's body. Animals become thirsty when their bodies need water, and this internal stimulus causes them to go find a cool drink someplace. You have certainly felt this way on a hot summer day! Plants do the same thing: As they grow larger, they send out longer roots to collect more water. Plants know to send their roots downward because they can sense gravity. Roots can sense water, as well, almost like an animal can smell food. This helps a plant grow toward water sources.

As you learned in Review 17, animals gather information about their environments with their senses (sight, hearing, smell, and so on). Animals use this information to respond to changes in their surroundings. For example, the skin responds to changes in temperature. Some animals perspire (sweat) when they get hot; others pant (heavy, open-mouthed breathing). When it gets too cold, many animals shiver. This helps keep the animal warm. As another example, consider how an animal might respond to a threat. If an animal sees, smells, or hears something dangerous, its heart might beat faster and its breathing might speed up. This prepares the animal to move quickly or react with more strength than usual. You may have heard the term "fight or flight." This is an **instinct**. When an animal gets scared, it responds by getting ready to run or put up a fight.

Changes in temperature, the smell of food, the sight of a dangerous animal— are these internal or external stimuli?

_____

You're probably quite familiar with one internal stimulus: hunger. Hunger is a message sent by your body to your brain that says, "Hey, I'm ready for some more energy!" Humans have figured out many ways to keep a steady supply of food coming in, and most of us eat three meals a day. As a result, we don't feel hunger all the time. Wild animals don't have it so easy, however, so they're almost constantly looking for their next meal. This is a response to an internal stimulus.

Plants seek out food, as well. Their leaves use sunlight to create sugars and starches. This is the start of almost all the food energy on Earth, something you'll learn more about in Review 20.

How do plants know the best direction to grow in order to get the most sunlight?

_____

_____

All of the living and nonliving things in an organism's environment affect it. Plants and animals react to these external stimuli every day. When everything in an environment affects every other thing the way it should, we say that the environment is in balance. This balance is sensitive to changes, and changes in nonliving things cause changes in the living things.

One important external stimulus that causes plants and animals to change is the presence of animals that want to eat that plant or animal. Plants have a wide variety of defenses against such animals. You've probably noticed the thorns on rosebushes and other types of plants. There is even a type of tree that has a motion detector: The mimosa tree will fold its leaves up when it senses leaf-eating insects crawling on it. The insects fall to the ground, still hungry.

Both plants and animals respond to changes in the weather. When it turns cold in autumn, a tree pulls its sap back into its trunk and roots to start saving energy for the winter. Some animals may go into **hibernation**, which is a period of very low activity (almost like sleeping) during the winter. Other animals will put on an extra layer of fat or grow thicker fur. A squirrel will start burying stashes of acorns. Your parents might put up special storm windows, or get the hats, coats, and mittens out from the basement. The weather is an example of an external stimulus.

What are some other external stimuli that cause changes in plants?

_____

_____

_____

Changes in environmental conditions often lead to changes in animal behavior. For example, when autumn turns into winter, polar bears travel onto the ice-covered waters of the Arctic Ocean to hunt seals. When spring arrives, they move back onto land. These seasonal movements are called **migrations**. Animals have different reasons for making migrations. Some migrate to avoid the cold weather; others move to avoid hot weather. One of the most common reasons for migrations is to reach a new source of food. The distances of many migrations are quite amazing. For example, the short-tailed shearwater is a type of bird that travels around the Pacific Ocean each year, flying an average distance of 32,000 km—almost 20,000 miles!

Use the library or the Internet to answer the following questions. What is another animal that makes a migration each year? Why does that animal migrate?

_____

_____

_____

_____

Over time, each organism becomes specially **adapted** to live in its particular environment. If the environment changes, the living things in it must also change, or they will die off and become **extinct**. If the changes to the environment are very slow, many organisms will be able to adapt and survive. But if the changes to the environment are very fast, the organisms will not be able to adapt, and they will become extinct.

Name some organisms that were unable to adapt and became extinct.

_____

_____

What will most likely happen if an environment changes, but a certain plant does not adapt?

_____

_____

_____

As you learned in Review 15, all organisms need food, water, and shelter for survival. An organism tries to fill these needs in its **habitat**. Sometimes a habitat doesn't have many **resources**, making it more difficult for an organism to survive. Other times, poor weather conditions or having many living things that are in **competition** for the same resources can reduce supplies and threaten survival in a certain habitat. In other words, the population of any organism is limited by the availability of resources in a given area.

What are some conditions that might limit resources or threaten survival for each of these living things?

Plants: _____

_____

Animals: _____

_____

Humans: _____

_____

Because organisms must compete for the limited resources within a habitat, not all organisms can survive. Many species become extinct because they cannot adapt to a change in their habitat, whether that change is a new competitor or a shift in the climate. On the other hand, those species that can adapt over time develop characteristics that help them survive. Organisms from these species are more likely to live long enough to reproduce, passing on their successful features to their offspring.

Using What You Know

Below are two lists, one of organisms, the other of nonliving environmental factors. Choose three organisms from the list, then choose a different nonliving environmental factor to go with each so that you have three different organism/ environmental factor pairs. Show your pairs by drawing a line from each of the organisms you selected to a different nonliving environmental factor. Discuss with a classmate how these pairs might illustrate a stimulus-response relationship.

Organism	Nonliving Environmental Factor
Flies	Hot weather
Frogs	Lots of rain
Raccoons	A snowstorm
Geese	Freezing temperatures
Ducks	Nighttime

What stimulus and response do you expect in your first pair?

_____

_____

_____

What stimulus and response do you expect in your second pair?

_____

_____

_____

What stimulus and response do you expect in your third pair?

_____

_____

_____

Think It Over

1. What kinds of behaviors would you expect from an earthworm when you shine a flashlight on it at night?

_____

_____

_____

2. Describe a way in which humans have learned to respond to each of the five environmental factors on the list on page 172.

_____

_____

_____

_____

_____

3. Describe how humans can benefit from studying the behaviors of organisms.

_____

_____

_____

_____

Practice Questions

1. To react to changes in its environment, an individual plant might do any of the following except which one?

   A. die

   B. grow

   C. adjust to the changes

   D. move to another area

2. Some animals respond to seasonal changes in weather by traveling great distances. Usually, these animals are looking for a new food source. What is the term for this seasonal travel?

   A. instinct

   B. camouflage

   C. migration

   D. hibernation

3. Which of the following is an example of a response to an internal stimulus?
   A. A flower turns toward the Sun.
   B. A bear searches for food in the morning.
   C. A snake finds a place to hibernate.
   D. A rabbit runs away from a fox.

4. When living things adapt, they change so that they can better survive in their environment. How quickly do physical adaptations usually happen?
   A. very quickly, taking about a year
   B. somewhat quickly, taking a few years
   C. very slowly, taking generations to show up
   D. somewhat slowly, occurring within a creature's life

Directions: Use the following pictures to answer Number 5.

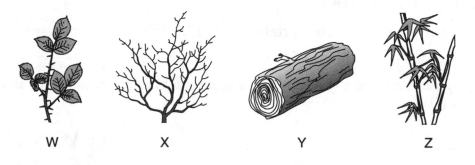

W   X   Y   Z

5. Which of these stems has the best defense against an animal eating its bark?
   A. W
   B. X
   C. Y
   D. Z

Review 20

Connections Among Living Things

At the start of the 20th century, fewer than 1 billion people lived on Earth. In the early part of the 21st century, there are more than 6 billion (6,000,000,000) people. Earth seems big enough to support more people, but no one is sure just how many more. And the more humans there are, the more damage is done to plants, animals, and ecosystems. How can we find the right balance? More and more, we are remembering that the human world is not separate from the plant and animal worlds: Humans cannot be healthy without a healthy population of plants and animals. This review will look at the ways in which plants and animals (including humans) interact with each other, and the ways in which living things react to a changing **environment**.

What Do You Think?

How many people could live comfortably on Earth? This is an important question for everyone.

If the population were to continue to increase, what are some things that there would need to be more of?

_____

_____

_____

_____

How do you think having more people affects other living and nonliving things?

_____

_____

_____

_____

_____

Key Words

carnivore

competition

consumer

cultivation

decomposer

environment

food chain

food web

herbivore

interdependency

omnivore

overpopulation

pollution

predator

prey

producer

scavenger

What People Think

In some way, every living thing on Earth depends on every other living thing to survive. This is called **interdependency**. In nature, examples of interdependency are easy to see. Some animals eat plants and some animals eat other animals. We call living things that kill and eat other living things **predators**; the living things that are killed and eaten are called **prey**. This interdependency of living things for food is called the **food chain**. All living things have their place in a food chain, and almost all food chains begin with the Sun. For example, the Sun provides the energy for a mulberry tree to produce leaves, which are eaten by a silkworm. A robin gobbles up the silkworm, and later a hawk swoops in and eats the robin. Because plants use the Sun's energy to produce food, they are called **producers**. Animals rely on plants for food, so they are called **consumers**.

Using your textbook or another book, find an example of each of the following:

Herbivore: _____

Carnivore: _____

Omnivore: _____

Not all parts of the food chain eat other living things. **Decomposers** perform a valuable job by consuming plant and animal matter after an organism dies. Decomposers (such as mushrooms, toadstools, and other fungi) are nature's recyclers: For all the dead organisms that they consume, they also bring that food energy back into the ecosystem. For example, decomposers make soil richer for plants, and many animals eat decomposers.

Not all examples of interdependency in nature involve food and eating. Many animals depend on plants that they do not eat for survival.

How do birds depend on trees? _____

_____

_____

_____

How do deer depend on trees? _____

_____

_____

_____

A food chain is a simple way to describe relationships between living things. The real world, however, is more complicated. For example, most organisms eat (or are eaten by) more than one thing. A habitat is typically made of many food chains. Taken together, multiple food chains are a **food web**. The following food web is based on a healthy grass population.

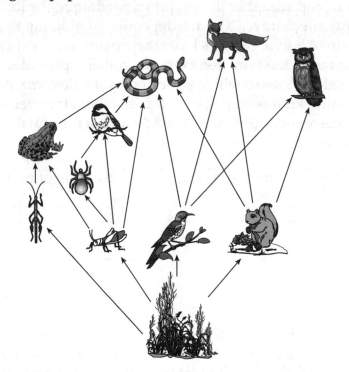

In this food web, how many animals consume the grasshopper?

_____

Predict what would happen to the ecosystem if the snake population disappeared.

_____

_____

As you learned in Review 19, plants and animals often try to get the same food, shelter, or other resource. This means that species are in **competition** for resources. For comparison, imagine two soccer teams: They compete with each other to fill the role of "winner." Similarly, two species often compete for food, water, shelter, or habitat. Members within a species often compete, as well. In nature, there aren't enough resources for all species to grow and grow endlessly. Competition keeps populations steady, and in this way it helps lead to a balanced environment.

Crows are one of the most successful birds in the United States. They are omnivores, which means they'll eat plants or animals. They are also **scavengers**, which means they'll eat the flesh from already-dead animals. What are some animals in your area that provide competition for the crow?

_____

_____

_____

_____

_____

Humans are one of the most successful species in the history of the Earth. One of the main reasons why humans have been so successful is because we have learned to change the environment to suit our needs. Thousands of years ago, our ancestors learned how to grow their own food, a practice called **cultivation**. Instead of searching for food all the time, humans could grow their own and store it over the winter. Humans began clearing forests to make room for growing crops and keeping animals.

Humans also change the environment by creating shelter. Other animals build simple structures, but humans create towns and cities that change hundreds of square kilometers of the environment. We have built roads, canals, railroads, and highways so we can move people and goods between towns and cities. Each one of these cuts apart a natural environment.

In the past 200 years, humans have been changing the environment more quickly than ever. Through technology, we have invented machines that can make things quickly. We dig mines to find valuable materials like coal, oil, gold, and iron. We cut down whole forests to get enough paper and building materials for our wants and needs.

All of these activities change the environment. The effect is made worse when the human population increases. As the graph below shows, the population of humans has skyrocketed in the past 200 years. This **overpopulation** is expected to get worse in the future. This huge population means that more land must be used for farming and shelter. Additionally, **pollution** (puh LOO shun) has become a major problem. Pollution is any material that causes harm to an environment. Human waste, smoke, chemicals, and other substances have threatened the water, air, and land all over the Earth.

World Population Growth

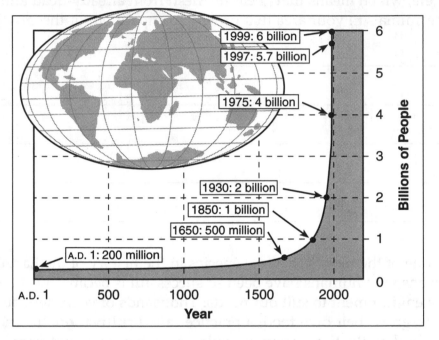

With the new technology and huge population produced during the last 200 years, the human need for energy has increased. We burn oil, coal, and natural gas to create heat for warmth and cooking and to drive our machines. All this burning gives off pollution. Cleaner options include solar power (using the Sun's energy for electricity) and wind power. It is important for us to reduce the damage we do to the environment. Remember the idea of interdependency: We are dependent on a healthy population of plants and animals. We need to reach a balance with the rest of life on Earth if all of us are to survive.

Using What You Know

The illustration below shows some living things that might be found in and around a wetlands area.

Step 1: Turn to page 203 and cut out the pond life cards.

Step 2: Arrange the cards on a large sheet of newsprint. Draw a large blue circle with a crayon to show the pond.

Step 3: Pick out the producers. Place the producers around the edge of the pond that you have just drawn.

Step 4: Choose one of the insects that eats or lives in one of those plants.

Step 5: Choose a second animal that eats the one that you picked in Step 4.

What is the term for this second animal?

_____

Step 6: Your teacher has put out different-colored yarns. Choose one color. Tape this color between the living things that you selected in Steps 3, 4, and 5. This is a food chain.

Step 7: Use different colors of yarn to create food chains for the remaining animals in your pond.

Think It Over

1. Cut the frog yarn and remove the frog card from your picture. What would happen to the mosquito population and raccoon population if the frog were gone?

   _____

   _____

   _____

   _____

2. Cut the duckweed yarn and remove the duckweed card from your picture. What will happen to the pond ecosystem if the duckweed dies off?

   _____

   _____

   _____

   _____

Practice Questions

Directions: The following illustration of a freshwater pond uses arrows to show what each thing eats. Use it to answer Numbers 1 and 2.

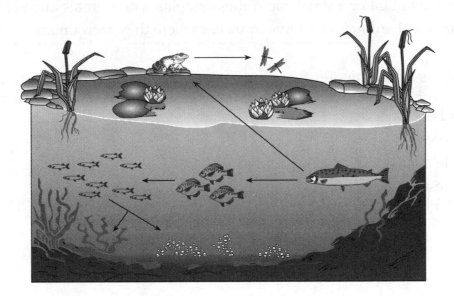

1. Which of the following statements best describes the relationship between the big and small fish?

   A. The big fish are prey, and the small fish are predators.

   B. The small fish are prey, and the big fish are predators.

   C. The big fish and the small fish are in different food chains.

   D. The small fish are predators, and the big fish are lower in the food chain.

2. If the plants in this pond disappeared, how might the other things be affected?

   _____

   _____

   _____

   _____

3. Why is it a bad idea to move plants or animals from one part of the world to another part of the world?

A. People might not like how the new plant or animal looks.

B. There are too few plants and animals to be taking any to new places.

C. The new plant or animal could threaten plants or animals already there.

D. Plants and animals can't live in places where they aren't naturally found.

4. Jackrabbits are herbivores that range over much of the southwestern United States. Which of the following would most likely compete with the jackrabbit for food?

A. coyotes

B. mule deer

C. rattlesnakes

D. turkey vultures

APPENDIX

Glossary

adapt: to develop characteristics that help an organism survive and reproduce in its environment (Review 19)

apparent motion: the illusion created by the Earth's rotation and revolution that makes it appear as though the Sun and the other stars are moving around the Earth (Review 7)

aquifer: a layer of rock, gravel, or sand that collects groundwater (Review 8)

atmosphere: the layer of gases surrounding the Earth that helps support life (Review 8)

axis: the imaginary line that connects the North and South Poles; the Earth rotates on its axis (Review 7)

bar graph: a picture used to compare data that can be put into separate groups (Review 4)

basic need: something that all living creatures must have in order to live: food, water, clean air, and shelter (Review 15)

behavior: any reaction of an animal to internal or external changes (Reviews 18, 19)

boil: to change from a liquid state to a gas state by adding heat energy (Review 11)

brainstorming web: a graphic organizer in which the main problem and possible solutions are placed in circles and connected by lines or arrows (Review 6)

camouflage: an adaptation that helps an organism blend in with its environment and be harder to see (Review 17)

carnivore: an animal that eats meat (Review 20)

cell: the smallest structure in a living thing (Review 15)

characteristic: a part, feature, or action of an animal, plant, or thing that can be used to compare it to other animals, plants, or things (Reviews 15, 18)

chemical energy: the energy that objects have because of the way their atoms are bonded together (Review 12)

circle graph: a diagram that shows how much of a whole that a certain part represents; also called a pie chart (Review 4)

claim: a statement that someone wants us to believe is true (Review 2)

closed circuit: a complete system of electrical parts in a path that is unbroken (Review 12)

competition: a relationship in which two living things (or groups of living things) try to get the same type of food, water, or shelter (Reviews 19, 20)

conclusion: a decision based on investigation and evidence (Review 4)

condense: to change from a gaseous state to a liquid state (Reviews 8, 11)

conduct: to carry electricity or heat (Review 10)

conductor: a material that can transfer heat or electricity easily (Review 12)

constraint: any limitation on a design; a constraint can be economic, material, social, or time-related (Review 6)

consumer: a living thing that gets its energy by eating other living things (Review 20)

contact force: a force that must touch an object to change its speed and/or direction (Review 14)

cost-benefit analysis: a process that compares the positive and negative factors of a technology (Review 5)

cultivation: the practice of growing plants and raising animals for food (Review 20)

data: information that describes events or things, such as temperatures or life spans (Reviews 2, 3)

decomposer: a living organism that breaks down dead organisms into smaller parts that can be reused by other living organisms (Review 20)

design: to plan out a solution (Review 6)

drug: a nonfood chemical substance that affects the way the body functions (Review 16)

drug abuse: excessive use of a drug for no acceptable medical reason (Review 16)

eclipse: an alignment of the Earth and the Moon so that one blocks sunlight from reaching the other (Review 7)

electricity: the energy of moving charges in atoms (Reviews 12, 13)

energy: the ability to cause change or to do work (Reviews 12, 13)

energy transformation: a change of energy into a different form, such as light energy changing to heat energy (Review 13)

engineer: one who identifies a problem in people's lives and designs a solution to that problem, often resulting in the creation of new technology (Review 6)

environment: all the living and nonliving things that surround and affect an organism (Reviews 18, 20)

erosion: the process in which small particles of soil and rock are carried away by glaciers, water, and wind (Review 9)

error: the difference between a measured value and an actual value (Review 3)

evaporate: to change from a liquid to a gas (Review 8)

evidence: data that can help explain or clarify something (Reviews 1, 2, 4)

experiment: a carefully planned activity done to help answer a question, test a hypothesis, or support an opinion (Review 1)

external stimulus: an environmental change that causes an organism to change its behavior; changes in temperature or the availability of food are examples of external stimuli (Review 19)

extinct: no longer existing as a species (Reviews 16, 19)

fact: a piece of information that can be proven to be true (Review 2)

fair test: an experiment that tests one variable and keeps all the other variables the same (Review 3)

flower: reproductive structure in some seed plants (Review 17)

food chain: a link from a lower organism (a plant, for example) to a higher organism (a rabbit) to a higher organism (a fox), and so on (Review 20)

food guide pyramid: a chart in the shape of a pyramid that shows what kinds of food groups there are and how much of each group we should eat every day (Review 16)

food web: a combination of food chains showing how different living things must balance each other in nature; also called "web of life" (Review 20)

force: a push or pull that causes something to change its speed or direction (Review 14)

forecast: to predict the weather; a weather prediction (Review 8)

fossil fuel: energy sources formed from the remains of once-living organisms; includes coal, oil, and natural gas (Review 13)

freeze: to change from a liquid state to a solid state (Review 11)

friction: the force that acts to slow the motion of the things that are moving (Review 14)

fruit: a plant body that holds and protects seeds (Review 17)

fulcrum: a point or support around which a lever rotates (Review 14)

gas: matter that does not have a definite shape or volume (Review 10)

glacier: a gigantic formation of ice that does not melt over the course of a year (Review 9)

global warming: the rise in global temperatures; although there is some debate, most scientists believe that it is caused by an increase in greenhouse gases from human pollution (Review 2)

graduated cylinder: a tall, narrow container used to measure liquids (Review 3)

graphic organizer: a combination of sketches, diagrams, and lists that helps engineers organize their design plan (Review 6)

gravity: a force that pulls two objects toward each other (Reviews 7, 14)

greenhouse effect: the warming of the Earth as a result of gases in the atmosphere that capture some of the Sun's heat reflected back from the Earth (Review 2)

groundwater: water located below ground that constitutes about 0.7% of Earth's water supply (Review 8)

habitat: the living environment that an organism requires to live (Review 19)

hardware: the equipment needed to run a computer (Review 5)

heat energy: the form of energy arising from the motion of all particles in a system (Review 12)

herbivore: an animal that eats only plants (Review 20)

hibernation: an adaptation in which an organism slows down during the winter (Review 19)

humidity: the amount of water vapor in the air (Review 8)

humus: partially decomposed plant or animal material that makes up part of the soil (Review 9)

hygiene: the practice of staying clean and healthy (Review 16)

hypothesis: a reasonable guess or possible explanation that can be tested (Review 2)

ice wedging: a type of physical weathering during which water freezes, expands, and creates cracks in rocks and rock-based materials (Review 9)

inherit: to receive characteristics passed from a parent to offspring through reproduction (Review 18)

inquiry: an examination, exploration, or investigation designed to solve a problem or answer a question (Review 1)

instinct: a behavior that animals are born knowing; behavior that is not taught (Reviews 18, 19)

instrument: a special tool used to make observations or measure things (Review 3)

insulator: a material that does not easily transfer heat or electricity (Review 12)

interdependency: the idea that every living thing on Earth depends on every other living thing to survive (Review 20)

internal stimulus: a change within an organism's body that causes a change in the organism's behavior; thirst and hunger are examples of internal stimuli (Review 19)

journal: a notebook in which a person writes down data (Review 4)

judgment: an opinion about what the best action or answer is (Review 2)

kinetic energy: the energy of moving things (Review 12)

larva: the second of four stages an insect goes through during metamorphosis; it follows the egg stage (Review 16)

leaf: plant organ that contains chlorophyll; the place where sunlight is absorbed and photosynthesis occurs (Review 17)

learned behavior: actions that are taught, often by parents to offspring (Review 18)

lever: a rigid object that rotates around a fulcrum (Review 14)

life cycle: a pattern of living things that involves birth, growth, reproduction, and death (Review 16)

light: a form of energy that allows us to see; used by plants to make food (Review 12)

line graph: a picture showing how data change over time (Review 4)

liquid: matter that has a definite volume but not a definite shape (Review 10)

living: being alive or showing signs of life; living things have cells, need food and water, grow, reproduce, and respond to changes in the environment (Review 15)

luminous: having the ability to give off light energy (Review 12)

machine: anything that helps you do work with less force or with greater speed (Review 14)

magnetism: the ability to attract certain metals, and to attract or repel other magnetic materials (Review 12)

map: a representation of an area on the Earth, in the sky, on the Moon, and so on (Review 4)

mass: the amount of matter in something (Review 10)

matter: the material from which all substances are made (Review 10)

mechanical energy: the energy of motion and of the position of things (Review 12)

medium: the substance through which a wave travels (Review 12)

melt: to change from a solid state to a liquid state (Review 11)

metamorphosis: the dramatic changes some organisms go through to become an adult (Review 16)

meteorologist: a scientist who studies the atmosphere (Review 8)

metric system: the system of measurement used by most nations and all scientists (Review 3)

migration: an instinctive behavior in some animals in which they travel long distances, usually for better feeding opportunities (Reviews 18, 19)

mixture: the combination of two different elements or compounds where the different substances keep their original properties (Review 11)

model: an object or explanation that represents and simplifies a system (Review 1)

motion: any change in an object's position over time (Review 14)

noncontact force: a force that acts on an object from a distance, such as gravity or magnetism (Review 14)

nonliving: never having been alive (Review 15)

nonrenewable energy: a resource that cannot be replaced by nature (Review 13)

nuclear energy: energy created by breaking apart or combining atoms (Review 13)

nutrient: a substance, such as vitamins, minerals, or water, needed for the healthy growth of living things (Review 15)

nutrition: the science of eating healthfully (Review 16)

observation: information gathered by the senses or through scientific measurements (Review 1)

offspring: the product of reproduction; the new organisms created by the parent organisms (Review 16)

omnivore: an animal that is both an herbivore and a carnivore, eating both plants and animals (Review 20)

open circuit: a system of electrical parts in a path that is broken or incomplete (Review 12)

opinion: a statement that cannot be proven and therefore cannot be the basis of scientific knowledge (Review 2)

orbit: the path of an object in space as it travels around another object (Review 7)

organism: a living being (Review 15)

overpopulation: a condition in which a population of organisms is so dense that it harms the organisms' environment and quality of life (Review 20)

pattern: a repetition in nature that helps us predict what will happen in the future (Review 2)

pendulum: an object that is hung from a fixed point and that can swing freely (Review 12)

phase: the different shapes of the Moon as it progresses through a one-month cycle, as seen from Earth (Review 7)

photosynthesis: the process by which plants make food from sunlight, water, and carbon dioxide (Review 17)

physical change: a change in the appearance, size, shape, or state of matter (Review 11)

pollen: a powdery substance that fertilizes flowers and causes seeds to form (Reviews 16, 17)

pollution: any harmful thing produced by humans that causes the environment to be unhealthy (Review 20)

potential energy: the energy of the position of matter (Review 12)

precipitation: water that falls from the clouds to the Earth; depending on the temperature, the water can be in the form of rain, hail, snow, and so on (Review 8)

predator: an animal that eats other animals (Reviews 17, 20)

prey: an animal that is eaten by other animals (Review 20)

producer: a living thing that changes the Sun's energy into food (Review 20)

property: a characteristic of an individual or thing; a trait (Review 10)

prototype: the first full-sized construction of a new idea, used to test a design and look for mistakes (Review 6)

pupa: the third stage of metamorphosis for some animals, after egg and larva, and before adult (Review 16)

reflection: the bouncing of light off of a surface (Review 12)

relative motion: an object's motion as it is compared with something else (Review 14)

renewable energy: a resource that can be replaced by nature (Review 13)

reproduce: to create offspring and begin a new generation (Review 16)

research: exploring ideas, searching for information, and forming hypotheses before beginning an experiment (Review 2)

resource: any material that helps a living thing meet a basic need (Review 19)

revolution: the movement of an object around another object; for example, it takes the Earth one year to make one revolution around the Sun (Review 7)

root: the part of the plant below ground that collects minerals and water and holds the plant in the soil (Review 17)

rotation: the spin of something on its axis; for example, it takes the Earth one day to make one rotation (Review 7)

runoff: water that runs over the land to waterways, being neither absorbed into the Earth nor evaporated into the air (Review 8)

scavenger: an organism that consumes the flesh of already-dead animals (Review 20)

seasons: the year-long cycle of temperature changes caused by the Earth's tilt as it revolves around the Sun (Review 7)

sediment: very small solid particles carried by wind, water, or ice and later deposited (Review 9)

seed: reproductive structure in some plants; contains plant embryo and food (Review 17)

shelter: protection against harmful things in the environment (Review 15)

simulation: an experiment, often done with computers, that models an actual event (Review 5)

society: a group of people having many common values, beliefs, traditions, and interests (Review 5)

software: the set of instructions that tells a computer what to do (Review 5)

solar energy: a form of energy that combines the properties of light and heat from the Sun (Review 12)

solar system: a set of planets, moons, asteroids, and comets that are held together by the gravity of a star (Review 7)

solid: matter that has both a definite volume and shape (Review 10)

sound: noise that is created by the rapid vibration of matter (Review 12)

species: a group of organisms sharing a set of characteristics and a specific group name (Review 16)

state: one of the forms in which matter exists, including solid, liquid, and gas (Review 11)

stem: plant structure that supports plants; conducts food, water, and minerals (Review 17)

stimulus: an environmental factor that causes a behavior (Review 19)

system: an organized group of related objects that form a whole (Review 1)

table: a drawing that uses rows and columns to organize large amounts of information (Review 4)

technology: the practical use of knowledge to design things that make people's lives better, easier, or safer (Review 5)

thrive: to grow and remain healthy (Review 15)

time: what flies when you're having fun (Review 7)

trait: a feature that an organism inherits from its parents (Review 18)

turbine: an engine that rotates in a magnetic field to make electricity (Review 13)

U.S. customary system: a system of weighing and measuring objects based on pounds and feet, commonly used in the United States for nonscientific purposes (Review 3)

variable: a factor that changes in an experiment (Reviews 2, 3)

variation: a difference between members of the same species due to genetic or environmental factors (Review 18)

vertebrate: an animal with a spinal column as a part of its skeletal system (Review 17)

vitamin: a substance needed by the body to grow and to function properly (Review 16)

volcano: a place in the Earth's crust that shoots out hot materials from inside the Earth (Review 9)

volume: the amount of space that something takes up (Review 10)

water cycle: a continuous movement of water from the Earth's surface to the air and back to the surface (Review 8)

water vapor: water in gaseous form (Reviews 8, 11)

weather: the atmospheric conditions at a given time (Review 8)

weathering: the process in which materials such as rock are broken down by things such as wind and water (Review 9)

New York Learning Standards and Process Skills for Elementary-Level Science

Blast Off on New York Science, Book 4, is based on the New York State Learning Standards for Mathematics, Science, and Technology (Standards 1, 2, 4, 6, and 7) and the Elementary Science Core Curriculum (Grades K–4). The workbook has been designed to provide review and practice in the skills tested by the New York Grade 4 Elementary-Level Science Test. The following table matches the learning standards with the *Blast Off* reviews in which they are addressed.

Standard 1—Analysis, Inquiry, and Design	Blast Off Review(s)
Mathematical Analysis	
M1.1 Use special mathematical notation and symbolism to communicate in mathematics and to compare and describe quantities, express relationships, and relate mathematics to their immediate environment.	4
M2.1 Use simple logical reasoning to develop conclusions, recognizing that patterns and relationships present in the environment assist them in reaching these conclusions.	2, 3, 7
M3.1 Explore and solve problems generated from school, home, and community situations, using concrete objects or manipulative materials when possible.	3, 6
Scientific Inquiry	
S1.1 Ask "why" questions in attempts to seek greater understanding concerning objects and events they have observed and heard about.	1
S1.2 Question the explanations they hear from others and read about, seeking clarification and comparing them with their own observations and understandings.	1
S1.3 Develop relationships among observations to construct descriptions of objects and events and to form their own tentative explanations of what they have observed.	2, 3
S2.1 Develop written plans for exploring phenomena or for evaluating explanations guided by questions or proposed explanations they have helped formulate.	2
S2.2 Share their research plans with others and revise them based on their suggestions.	2
S2.3 Carry out their plans for exploring phenomena through direct observation and through the use of simple instruments that permit measurement of quantities, such as length, mass, volume, temperature, and time.	2, 3, 4
S3.1 Organize observations and measurements of objects and events through classification and the preparation of simple charts and tables.	4, 6
S3.2 Interpret organized observations and measurements, recognizing simple patterns, sequences, and relationships.	3, 4
S3.3 Share their findings with others and actively seek their interpretations and ideas.	4
S3.4 Adjust their explanations and understandings of objects and events based on their findings and new ideas.	1, 2, 4

Standard 1—Analysis, Inquiry, and Design *(Continued)*	*Blast Off* Review(s)
Engineering Design	
T1.1 Describe objects, imaginary or real, that might be modeled or made differently and suggest ways in which the objects can be changed, fixed, or improved.	6
T1.2 Investigate prior solutions and ideas from books, magazines, family, friends, neighbors, and community members.	6
T1.3 Generate ideas for possible solutions, individually and through group activity; apply age-appropriate mathematics and science skills; evaluate the ideas and determine the best solution; and explain reasons for the choices.	6
T1.4 Plan and build, under supervision, a model of the solution, using familiar materials, processes, and hand tools.	6
T1.5 Discuss how best to test the solution; perform the test under teacher supervision; record and portray results through numerical and graphic means; discuss orally why things worked or didn't work; and summarize results in writing, suggesting ways to make the solution better.	6
Standard 2—Information Systems	
• use computer technology, traditional paper-based resources, and interpersonal discussions to learn, do, and share science in the classroom	5
• select appropriate hardware and software that aids in word processing, creating databases, telecommunications, graphing, data display, and other tasks	5
• use information technology to link the classroom to world events	5
• use a variety of media to access scientific information	2, 5
• consult several sources of information and points of view before drawing conclusions	2
• identify and report sources in oral and written communications	2
• distinguish fact from fiction (presenting opinion as fact is contrary to the scientific process)	2, 4
• demonstrate an ability to critically evaluate information and misinformation	4
• recognize the impact of information technology on the daily life of students	5
Standard 6—Interconnectedness: Common Themes	
Systems Thinking	
• observe and describe interactions among components of simple systems	1
• identify common things that can be considered to be systems (e.g., a plant, a transportation system, human beings)	1
Models	
• analyze, construct, and operate models in order to discover attributes of the real thing	1
• discover that a model of something is different from the real thing but can be used to study the real thing	1, 4
• use different types of models, such as graphs, sketches, diagrams, and maps, to represent various aspects of the real world	4
Magnitude and Scale	
• observe that things in nature and things that people make have very different sizes, weights, and ages	3
• recognize that almost anything has limits on how big or small it can be	6

Standard 6—Interconnectedness: Common Themes *(Continued)*	*Blast Off* Review(s)
Equilibrium and Stability	
• observe that things change in some ways and stay the same in some ways	1
• recognize that things can change in different ways such as size, weight, color, and movement. Some small changes can be detected by taking measurements.	3
Patterns of Change	
• use simple instruments to measure such quantities as distance, size, and weight and look for patterns in the data	3
• analyze data by making tables and graphs and looking for patterns of change	3, 4
Optimization	
• choose the best alternative of a set of solutions under given constraints	2, 6
• explain the criteria used in selecting a solution orally and in writing	2, 6
Standard 7—Interdisciplinary Problem Solving	
Connections	
• analyze science/technology/society problems and issues that affect their home, school, or community, and carry out a remedial course of action	5
• make informed consumer decisions by applying knowledge about the attributes of particular products and making cost/benefit trade-offs to arrive at an optimal choice	2, 5
• design solutions to problems involving a familiar and real context, investigate related science concepts to determine the solution, and use mathematics to model, quantify, measure, and compute	6
• observe phenomena and evaluate them scientifically and mathematically by conducting a fair test of the effect of variables and using mathematical knowledge and technological tools to collect, analyze, and present data and conclusions	2, 3, 4
Strategies	
• work effectively • gather and process information • generate and analyze ideas • observe common themes • realize ideas • present results	throughout
Standard 4—The Physical Setting	
1.1: **Describe patterns of daily, monthly, and seasonal changes in their environment.**	
1.1a Natural cycles and patterns include: • Earth spinning around once every 24 hours (rotation), resulting in day and night • Earth moving in a path around the Sun (revolution), resulting in one Earth year • the length of daylight and darkness varying with the seasons • weather changing from day to day and through the seasons • the appearance of the Moon changing as it moves in a path around Earth to complete a single cycle	7
1.1b Humans organize time into units based on natural motions of Earth: • second, minute, hour • week, month	7
1.1c The Sun and other stars appear to move in a recognizable pattern both daily and seasonally.	7

Standard 4—The Physical Setting *(Continued)*	*Blast Off* Review(s)
2.1: **Describe the relationship among air, water, and land on Earth.**	
2.1a Weather is the condition of the outside air at a particular moment.	8
2.1b Weather can be described and measured by: • temperature • wind speed and direction • form and amount of precipitation • general sky conditions (cloudy, sunny, partly cloudy)	8
2.1c Water is recycled by natural processes on Earth. • evaporation: changing of water (liquid) into water vapor (gas) • condensation: changing of water vapor (gas) into water (liquid) • precipitation: rain, sleet, snow, hail • runoff: water flowing on Earth's surface • groundwater: water that moves downward into the ground	8
2.1d Erosion and deposition result from the interaction among air, water, and land. • interaction between air and water breaks down earth materials • pieces of earth material may be moved by air, water, wind, and gravity • pieces of earth material will settle or deposit on land or in the water in different places • soil is composed of broken-down pieces of living and nonliving earth material	9
2.1e Extreme natural events (floods, fires, earthquakes, volcanic eruptions, hurricanes, tornadoes, and other severe storms) may have positive or negative impacts on living things.	8, 9
3.1: **Observe and describe properties of materials, using appropriate tools.**	
3.1a Matter takes up space and has mass. Two objects cannot occupy the same place at the same time.	10
3.1b Matter has properties (color, hardness, odor, sound, taste, etc.) that can be observed through the senses.	10
3.1c Objects have properties that can be observed, described, and/or measured: length, width, volume, size, shape, mass or weight, temperature, texture, flexibility, reflectiveness of light.	10
3.1d Measurements can be made with standard metric units and nonstandard units. *(Note: Exceptions to the metric system usage are found in meteorology.)*	3, 10
3.1e The material(s) an object is made up of determine some specific properties of the object (sink/float, conductivity, magnetism). Properties can be observed or measured with tools such as hand lenses, metric rulers, thermometers, balances, magnets, circuit testers, and graduated cylinders.	10
3.1f Objects and/or materials can be sorted or classified according to their properties.	10
3.1g Some properties of an object are dependent on the conditions of the present surroundings in which the object exists. For example: • temperature – hot or cold • lighting – shadows, color • moisture – wet or dry	10

Standard 4—The Physical Setting *(Continued)*	*Blast Off* Review(s)
3.2: Describe chemical and physical changes, including changes in states of matter.	
3.2a Matter exists in three states: solid, liquid, gas. • solids have a definite shape and volume • liquids do not have a definite shape but have a definite volume • gases do not hold their shape or volume	11
3.2b Temperature can affect the state of matter of a substance.	11
3.2c Changes in the properties or materials of objects can be observed and described.	11
4.1: Describe a variety of forms of energy (e.g., heat, chemical, light) and the changes that occur in objects when they interact with those forms of energy.	
4.1a Energy exists in various forms: heat, electric, sound, chemical, mechanical, light.	12
4.1b Energy can be transferred from one place to another.	13
4.1c Some materials transfer energy better than others (heat and electricity).	12
4.1d Energy and matter interact: water is evaporated by the Sun's heat; a bulb is lighted by means of electrical current; a musical instrument is played to produce sound; dark colors may absorb light, light colors may reflect light.	13
4.1e Electricity travels in a closed circuit.	12
4.1f Heat can be released in many ways, for example, by burning, rubbing (friction), or combining one substance with another.	12
4.1g Interactions with forms of energy can be either helpful or harmful.	13
4.2: Observe the way one form of energy can be transferred into another form of energy present in common situations (e.g., mechanical to heat energy, mechanical to electrical energy, chemical to heat energy).	
4.2a Everyday events involve one form of energy being changed to another. • animals convert food to heat and motion • the Sun's energy warms the air and water	13
4.2b Humans utilize interactions between matter and energy. • chemical to electrical, light, and heat: battery and bulb • electrical to sound (e.g., doorbell buzzer) • mechanical to sound (e.g., musical instruments, clapping) • light to electrical (e.g., solar-powered calculator)	13
5.1: Describe the effects of common forces (pushes and pulls) of objects, such as those caused by gravity, magnetism, and mechanical forces.	
5.1a The position of an object can be described by locating it relative to another object or the background (e.g., on top of, next to, over, under, etc.).	14
5.1b The position or direction of motion of an object can be changed by pushing or pulling.	14
5.1c The force of gravity pulls objects toward the center of Earth.	14
5.1d The amount of change in the motion of an object is affected by friction.	14
5.1e Magnetism is a force that may attract or repel certain materials.	12, 14
5.1f Mechanical energy may cause change in motion through the application of force and through the use of simple machines such as pulleys, levers, and inclined planes.	14

Standard 4—The Physical Setting *(Continued)*	Blast Off Review(s)
5.2: **Describe how forces can operate across distances.**	
5.2a The forces of gravity and magnetism can affect objects through gases, liquids, and solids.	14
5.2b The force of magnetism on objects decreases as distance increases.	14
Standard 4—The Living Environment	
1.1: **Describe the characteristics of and variations between living and nonliving things.**	
1.1a Animals need air, water, and food in order to live and thrive.	15
1.1b Plants require air, water, nutrients, and light in order to live and thrive.	15
1.1c Nonliving things do not live and thrive.	15
1.1d Nonliving things can be human-created or naturally occurring.	15
1.2: **Describe the life processes common to all living things.**	
1.2a Living things grow, take in nutrients, breathe, reproduce, eliminate waste, and die.	15
2.1: **Recognize that traits of living things are both inherited and acquired or learned.**	
2.1a Some traits of living things have been inherited (e.g., color of flowers and number of limbs of animals).	18
2.1b Some characteristics result from an individual's interactions with the environment and cannot be inherited by the next generation (e.g., having scars; riding a bicycle).	18
2.2: **Recognize that for humans and other living things there is genetic continuity between generations.**	
2.2a Plants and animals closely resemble their parents and other individuals in their species.	18
2.2b Plants and animals can transfer specific traits to their offspring when they reproduce.	18
3.1: **Describe how the structures of plants and animals complement the environment of the plant or animal.**	
3.1a Each animal has different structures that serve different functions in growth, survival, and reproduction.	17
3.1b Each plant has different structures that serve different functions in growth, survival, and reproduction.	17
3.1c In order to survive in their environment, plants and animals must be adapted to that environment.	17
3.2: **Observe that differences within a species may give individuals an advantage in surviving and reproducing.**	
3.2a Individuals within a species may compete with each other for food, mates, space, water, and shelter in their environment.	19
3.2b All individuals have variations, and because of these variations, individuals of a species may have an advantage in surviving and reproducing.	18, 19, 20

Standard 4—The Living Environment *(Continued)*	Blast Off Review(s)
4.1: **Describe the major stages in the life cycles of selected plants and animals.**	
4.1a Plants and animals have life cycles. These may include beginning of a life, development into an adult, reproduction as an adult, and eventually death.	16
4.1b Each kind of plant goes through its own stages of growth and development that may include seed, young plant, and mature plant.	16
4.1c The length of time from beginning of development to death of the plant is called its life span.	16
4.1d Life cycles of some plants include changes from seed to mature plant.	16
4.1e Each generation of animals goes through changes in form from young to adult. This completed sequence of changes in form is called a life cycle. Some insects change from egg to larva to pupa to adult.	16
4.1f Each kind of animal goes through its own stages of growth and development during its life span.	16
4.1g The length of time from an animal's birth to its death is called its life span. Life spans of different animals vary.	16
4.2: **Describe evidence of growth, repair, and maintenance, such as nails, hair, and bone, and the healing of cuts and bruises.**	
4.2a Growth is the process by which plants and animals increase in size.	16
4.2b Food supplies the energy and materials necessary for growth and repair.	16
5.1: **Describe basic life functions of common living specimens (e.g., guppies, mealworms, gerbils).**	
5.1a All living things grow, take in nutrients, breathe, reproduce, and eliminate waste.	15
5.1b An organism's external physical features can enable it to carry out life functions in its particular environment.	17
5.2: **Describe some survival behaviors of common living specimens.**	
5.2a Plants respond to changes in their environment. For example, the leaves of some green plants change position as the direction of light changes; the parts of some plants undergo seasonal changes that enable the plant to grow; seeds germinate, and leaves form and grow.	19
5.2b Animals respond to change in their environment, (e.g., perspiration, heart rate, breathing rate, eye blinking, shivering, and salivating).	19
5.2c Senses can provide essential information (regarding danger, food, mates, etc.) to animals about their environment.	19
5.2d Some animals, including humans, move from place to place to meet their needs.	17, 18, 19
5.2e Particular animal characteristics are influenced by changing environmental conditions including: fat storage in winter, coat thickness in winter, camouflage, shedding of fur.	19
5.2f Some animal behaviors are influenced by environmental conditions. These behaviors may include: nest building, hibernating, hunting, migrating, and communicating.	19
5.2g The health, growth, and development of organisms are affected by environmental conditions such as the availability of food, air, water, space, shelter, heat, and sunlight.	15, 16, 19

Standard 4—The Living Environment *(Continued)*	*Blast Off* Review(s)
5.3: **Describe the factors that help promote good health and growth in humans.**	
5.3a Humans need a variety of healthy foods, exercise, and rest in order to grow and maintain good health.	16
5.3b Good health habits include hand washing and personal cleanliness; avoiding harmful substances (including alcohol, tobacco, illicit drugs); eating a balanced diet; engaging in regular exercise.	16
6.1: **Describe how plants and animals, including humans, depend upon each other and the nonliving environment.**	
6.1a Green plants are producers because they provide the basic food supply for themselves and animals.	20
6.1b All animals depend on plants. Some animals (predators) eat other animals (prey).	20
6.1c Animals that eat plants for food may in turn become food for other animals. This sequence is called a food chain.	20
6.1d Decomposers are living things that play a vital role in recycling nutrients.	20
6.1e An organism's pattern of behavior is related to the nature of that organism's environment, including the kinds and numbers of other organisms present, the availability of food and other resources, and the physical characteristics of the environment.	19
6.1f When the environment changes, some plants and animals survive and reproduce, and others die or move to new locations.	19, 20
6.2: **Describe the relationship of the Sun as an energy source for living and nonliving cycles.**	
6.2a Plants manufacture food by utilizing air, water, and energy from the Sun.	20
6.2b The Sun's energy is transferred on Earth from plants to animals through the food chain.	20
6.2c Heat energy from the Sun powers the water cycle.	7
7.1: **Identify ways in which humans have changed their environment and the effects of those changes.**	
7.1a Humans depend on their natural and constructed environments.	20
7.1b Over time humans have changed their environment by cultivating crops and raising animals, creating shelter, using energy, manufacturing goods, developing means of transportation, changing populations, and carrying out other activities.	20
7.1c Humans, as individuals or communities, change environments in ways that can be either helpful or harmful for themselves and other organisms.	2, 20

Pond Life Cards

Use for "Using What You Know" activity on page 181.